W9-CSG-684

Design, Testing, and Optimization of Trading Systems

WILEY TRADER'S ADVANTAGE SERIES

John F. Ehlers, *MESA and Trading Market Cycles*
Robert Pardo, *Design, Testing, and Optimization of Trading Systems*

Design, Testing, and Optimization of Trading Systems

Robert Pardo

Series Editor: Perry J. Kaufman

John Wiley & Sons, Inc.

New York • Chichester • Brisbane • Toronto • Singapore

To Edward Pardo (1/16/1908–10/10/91)
Thanks Dad for always believing in and trusting me.

To Nora Pardo
I couldn't have done it without your steadfast support
and encouragement.

To Chris and Katie Pardo
Thanks for renewing my life and views with your
boundless curiosity, enthusiasm, and love.

In recognition of the importance of preserving what has been written, it is a policy of John Wiley & Sons, Inc., to have books of enduring value published in the United States printed on acid-free paper, and we exert our best efforts to that end.

This publication is designed to provide accurate and authoritative information in regard to the subject matter covered. It is sold with the understanding that the publisher is not engaged in rendering legal, accounting, or other professional services. If legal advice or other expert assistance is required, the services of a competent professional person should be sought. *From a Declaration of Principles jointly adopted by a Committee of the American Bar Association and a Committee of Publishers.*

Library of Congress Cataloging-in-Publication Data:

Pardo, Robert, 1951–
    Design, testing, and optimization of trading systems / by Robert Pardo.
        p.   cm.—(Wiley trader's library)
    ISBN 0-471-55446-4 (alk. paper)
    1. Futures—Data processing.   2. Options (Finance)—Data processing.   I. Title.   II. Series.
    HG4515.5.P37   1992
    332.64′5—dc20   92-372

Printed in the United States of America

10 9 8 7 6 5 4 3 2

ACKNOWLEDGMENTS

I would like to thank Bo Thunman, the editor of Club 3000 News, for getting the "ball moving" on this book originally. More importantly, I would like to thank him for the countless hours of conversation over the years exploring an endless succession of trading ideas and for his support and friendship. It has meant a lot to me.

I owe my series editor, Perry Kaufman, a special thanks. His book *Commodity Trading Systems and Methods,* above all others, provided inspiration at the beginning of my study of technical analysis. Our numerous conversations about the book proved thought-provoking and valuable. This book would not be the same without the careful craftsmanship he showed in its editing.

I also owe a note of thanks to Frank Martino my chief programmer. Frank has been one of the key translators of my trading and computer ideas into programs and a major sounding board for trading ideas over the years. Last but not least, he has been a loyal and dedicated employee and a good friend.

I would also like to acknowledge a former business associate Andrew Dziedzic. Over the years, we enjoyed countless conversations about the horizons of technical analysis. His open-minded and objective approach to trading and market analysis was always refreshing. His untimely death is not only a human tragedy but a loss to technical trading.

A special note of thanks to Steve Hendel who supported our endeavors.

Wendy Grau, my editor, Linda Indig, my production manager, and Nancy Land of Publications Development Company of Texas, have provided patience, support, and inspiration.

Thanks to Jim Hawkins and Rick Redmont for conversations over the years and for comments on a preliminary draft of this book.

THE TRADER'S ADVANTAGE SERIES PREFACE

The Trader's Advantage Series is a new concept in publishing for traders and analysts of futures, options, equity, and generally all world economic markets. Books in the series present single ideas with only that background information needed to understand the content. No long introductions, no definitions of the futures contract, clearing house, and order entry. Focused.

The futures and options industry is no longer in its infancy. From its role as an agricultural vehicle it has become the alterego of the most active world markets. The use of EFPs (exchange for physicals) in currency markets makes the selection of physical or futures markets transparent, in the same way the futures markets evolved into the official pricing vehicle for world grain. With a single telephone call, a trader or investment manager can hedge a stock portfolio, set a crossrate, perform a swap, or buy the protection of an inflation index. The classic regimes can no longer be clearly separated.

And this is just the beginning. Automated exchanges are penetrating traditional open outcry markets. Even now, from the time the transaction is completed in the pit, everything else is electronic. "Program trading" is the automated response to the analysis of a computerized ticker tape, and it is just the tip of the inevitable evolutionary process. Soon the executions will be computerized and then we won't be able to call anyone to complain about a fill. Perhaps we won't even have to place an order to get a fill.

Market literature has also evolved. Many of the books written on trading are introductory. Even those intended for more advanced audiences often include a review of contract specifications and market mechanics. There are very few books specifically targeted for the experienced and professional traders and analysts. *The Trader's Advantage Series* changes all that.

This series presents contributions by established professionals and exceptional research analysts. The authors' highly specialized talents have been applied primarily to futures, cash, and equity markets but are often generally applicable to price forecasting. Topics in the series will include trading systems and individual techniques, but all are a necessary part of the development process that is intrinsic to improving price forecasting and trading.

These works are creative, often state-of-the-art. They offer new techniques, in-depth analysis of current trading methods, or innovative and enlightening ways of looking at still unsolved problems. The ideas are explained in a clear, straightforward manner with frequent examples and illustrations. Because they do not contain unnecessary background material they are short and to the point. They require careful reading, study, and consideration. In exchange, they contribute knowledge to help build an unparalleled understanding of all areas of market analysis and forecasting.

PERRY J. KAUFMAN

Bermuda
July 1992

FOREWORD

Bob Pardo has been working on optimization problems for years. As the author of a general purpose test program, *Advanced Trader,* and the developer of numerous trading strategies, he has exactly the necessary credentials to view the optimization process from all sides—development, testing, and results.

At first, the use of the optimization methodology seems to be the simple, ideal solution to finding a successful trading system. But as you move through the steps, it becomes clear that there are serious, difficult decisions to be made.

The practical side of testing is the need to know how a set of rules and calculations (a strategy) would have performed had it been traded in the past. Because the formation of most methods comes from a review of past situations (either very specific situations or a generalized concept), it is only natural to want to see whether your perception of what would have happened is correct. It is perfectly justifiable to back-test your ideas. It would be more unreasonable to trade a strategy without knowing its likelihood of success, your risk exposure, and consequently the amount of capital needed to achieve the desired results.

Philosophically, there is another problem. The power of computers makes it possible to test so many combinations of patterns, rules, and formulas that there is little doubt a seemingly successful strategy will be found. Experience now shows that these solutions do not lead to real trading profits. The phenomenon, more recently understood as "overfitting," presents a dilemma for anyone developing a trading program. Bob Pardo addresses this problem directly, offering procedures and clear explanations of the correct solution.

The evaluation of optimization results must also be statistically sound. Presenting and interpreting the results properly is the key to finding the best solutions. The author understands this and shows when the pitfalls lead to unreliable results and market losses, while the correct process gives meaningful answers.

Anyone planning to use a computer to develop or verify a trading method should first read and understand this book.

PERRY J. KAUFMAN

Bermuda
July 1992

CONTENTS

1

ON OPTIMIZATION

Mechanical trading systems have been around as long as the markets. Interest in technical methods and trading systems tends to wax and wane with interest in the markets themselves. In the past 10 years, interest in trading systems has enjoyed tremendous growth. This development is largely due to the explosive growth in inexpensive computing power, which, in turn, has brought about an equal growth in the power and availability of sophisticated trading and testing software. The collaboration of all these trends has produced a renaissance in technical trading methods.

The combination of inexpensive computing power, sophisticated software, and a growing body of trading methods has now made it possible for the knowledgeable investor to design and test trading strategies on a par with professional investment firms. In fact, the capabilities of the contemporary investor equipped with testing software and a 486 computer far exceed that of a professional systems analyst working in 1975. In addition, the availability, range, and sophistication of current technical methods are also many times greater.

However, a thorough understanding of the proper design and testing of mechanical strategies has not kept pace with the growth in computing power, software, and technical methods. The life cycle of a successful trading strategy begins as an idea and ends in profit. This book presents the techniques required to design, test, optimize, and trade mechanical strategies.

The benefit of an accurately tested mechanical strategy is trading profit. The drawbacks of an improperly tested strategy are many; however, the primary one is trading losses. To add insult to injury, these losses are often preceded by many hours of labor and followed by the attendant frustration and disappointment that naturally result from such a failure.

The use of technical analysis and mechanical trading strategies has become widespread and continues to grow. By their nature, these numeric approaches to trading lend themselves to computerized testing. If done correctly, testing can add tremendous value to a trading strategy. Done incorrectly, it will lead to real-time trading losses. Consequently, the severity of the results of error means that computer testing must be done properly or not at all.

Ignorance of proper testing procedures has caused some traders to become disillusioned with computer testing. This ignorance has unjustly diminished the reputation of testing and optimization in some circles.

This book demonstrates that the benefits of correct testing and optimization vastly outweigh the effort required to learn their proper use. It sets forth in detail the correct way to formulate, test, and optimize a trading strategy. To set the record straight, this book makes a clear distinction between optimization, which is correct testing, and overfitting, which is incorrect testing. This book will explain, clarify, and illustrate:

- How to design, test, optimize, and evaluate a trading strategy.
- How properly to optimize a trading strategy.
- The symptoms of overfitting and guidelines to avoid it.
- What to expect from a trading model in real-time trading.
- How to judge real-time trading performance with respect to historical testing performance.

It is my hope that this book holds value for anyone who wishes to employ mechanical strategies in their trading. It presents from start to finish, the methods that must be employed to enjoy the fruits of a trading strategy.

A thorough review of strategy testing highlights one of its greatest benefits: the measurement of profit and risk. The value of a trading strategy must be evaluated in two interrelated dimensions: profit and risk. These two poles of trading performance cannot be judged in isolation; they can only be judged with respect to each other.

Therefore, a trading strategy can only be properly evaluated when profit and risk have been measured precisely. Profit and risk can only be measured through exhaustive computerized testing. These facts heighten the necessity of the computer testing of a trading strategy.

This book holds value for any trader, computerized or not. It presents the case for proper testing of a clearly specified trading strategy and offers refinements for the skills of the computerized trader. The noncomputer trader may acquire a first appreciation of the benefits of this trading approach.

Most definitely, anyone who is using computer-tested strategies and is not trading profitably should read this book, as should anyone who wants to make a start at strategy testing. A study of the guidelines presented herein will help determine and eliminate the causes of failure: a poor strategy, improper testing methodology, or incorrect real-time interpretation.

Again, at the risk of presumption, I believe that this book will help those computer traders out there who have been enjoying trading profit as a result of their work. A number of testing guidelines are presented that have yet to be put on paper. I hope that the detailed presentation of walk-forward analysis will bring this powerful methodology before the eyes of those who will use it to further enhance their trading profit.

THE BENEFITS OF COMPUTERIZED TESTING

The first reason to test a strategy is to see if it works. Testing a trading strategy correctly is a complicated procedure. Understanding if a trading strategy "works" in real-time trading is also moderately complex. This book shows how to make these two decisions, which are essential to profitable computerized trading.

The second reason to test a strategy is to arrive at a reliable measurement of its profit potential and its risk. The profit motive is what drives the trader to trade. However, it is the size of the risk that tells the trader how much it is going to cost to achieve this profit.

THE BENEFITS OF OPTIMIZATION

Once real-time trading has begun, the strategy must be kept current and constantly monitored. It is a fact of trading life that markets change. Trends change. Volatility and liquidity change. New types of conditions arise. These events may affect trading performance. One function of optimization is to maintain peak performance in a trading strategy in the face of continual change. Another function is to provide the measurements necessary to judge real-time performance.

Optimization can also adapt a trading strategy to different markets. All markets have their own unique personalities. A trading strategy may perform well in one market with one set of values and poorly in another with those same values. Optimization finds the best set of values for each market.

Different traders have different trading capital, time available, profit requirements, and predispositions to risk. Optimization adapts the trading strategy as much as possible to the needs of the trader.

OVERVIEW OF CHAPTERS

All things created by humans begin with an idea. An idea at its inception is likely to be vague. As the idea is considered further, it becomes more precise. As it becomes more precise, it takes on a more definite and concrete form. Once formulated in such a way, an idea is capable of becoming a reality.

The same holds true for a trading strategy. Chapter 2 maps out the seven steps through which a trading strategy must evolve beginning with formulation, continuing with testing, and ending with real-time trading. A mechanical trading strategy, as its name implies, is a set of objective rules external to the trader. All successful traders employ a consistent set of rules. The use of trading rules is essential to the management of risk.

Chapter 3 has two main parts. The first part presents the rationale for and the benefits that accrue from trading systems. The second part presents the seven major components of mechanical trading strategies and their uses. The prudent, contemporary trader is well aware that it is a great deal cheaper and much easier on the nervous system to evaluate the performance of a trading system using computer simulation instead of trading capital.

The evaluation of a trading strategy involves a number of different steps that build on each other. Chapter 4 presents the various issues that must be addressed to achieve the most accurate and realistic simulation of trading. The results of a trading simulation are based on selection criteria. There is an old saying, "Be careful of what you ask for, you just might get it." This is never more true than in simulation. Simulation work by its nature is very intensive computationally. Various ways of searching through a large number of simulations have been developed to reduce the amount of processing time required of simulations.

Chapter 5 explores the impact of different search and evaluation methods on test results. Different types of search and evaluation methods are presented with their strengths and weaknesses.

Chapter 6 presents preliminary testing as the first step in the evaluation of any trading strategy. This step verifies that the strategy has been correctly specified. The next level tests the strategy over a number of different markets and time periods. Of course, if the trading strategy has no variables, then it will not require optimization.

Many trading systems do have rules and formulas that can vary with different types of markets and conditions. Such a trading strategy will often benefit from optimization, which is used to determine the proper values for the trading system variables.

Chapter 7 presents the proper way to optimize a trading system. Optimization proceeds through two levels. The first is an optimization of the trading strategy over a variety of different markets and time periods. The optimization process is completed with an exhaustive walk-forward analysis that judges trading performance exclusively on the basis of out-of-sample trading.

After the trading strategy has been tested, optimized, and walked forward, it must be judged on its merits as an investment competing for capital within the universe of all investments as well as with other trading strategies. The performance of the trading strategy must also be judged on the basis of its internal structure. These two important topics are discussed in Chapter 8.

Because proper testing and optimization procedures are not well known by the trading community at large, the reputation of optimization has been somewhat diminished in some circles by its false association with overfitting.

Chapter 9 points out that the overfitting of a trading strategy to historical data occurs when testing and optimization are done incorrectly. To emphasize this fact, an entire chapter is dedicated to identifying the symptoms that result from the abuse of proper testing and optimization methods.

The goal of any strategy is trading profit. Once the full cycle of trading strategy evaluation has been successfully completed—namely, strategy formulation, testing, optimization, walk-forward analysis, and evaluation—real-time trading can begin.

Improper methods of evaluating real-time performance have caused problems for the computer trader. The only way that real-time trading performance can be judged is with respect to expectations created by proper testing.

Chapter 10 presents the guidelines that must be followed to assess real-time trading performance in the context of the knowledge of profit and risk arrived at by computer testing.

2

TRADING SYSTEM DEVELOPMENT

The development of a trading system is a complex process consisting of several interrelated steps. The entire procedure is quite straightforward if the trader performs each step carefully and thoroughly with proper attention to its significance.

There are two approaches to trading system development. The first approach applies reason and systematic, empirical verification; that is, each step must make sense before thorough testing begins. This approach, which is the one presented and developed in this book, is the path of knowledge. The profitable trading models that emerge from this approach offer an invaluable benefit. The trader of such a system has a complete understanding of why and how the trading model operates and is successful.

A simple example of this approach would proceed as follows. A theory of market action is developed, such as that an expansion of the daily range predicts a change in trend. A mechanism to use this theory to trade is designed. Go long when the market rallies 120% of the 3-day average daily range from yesterday's close. Go short when the market falls 120% of the 3-day average daily range from yesterday's close. Exit on opposite signals. A program is written to test this idea. It is found to be modestly profitable over five markets in five historical periods.

Optimization and walk-forward testing uncover the full scope of its profitability. It is found to be sound. It is traded in real time. Real-time performance is consistent with test performance. Trading continues. Refinement of the system continues.

A thorough understanding of the trading model has many benefits. The most important are these:

- It is much easier to make improvements to the system over time.
- It is much easier to stick with the system in its inevitable lean periods.

Without an understanding of the theoretical foundation of the model, sticking with and improving a system become very difficult.

The second approach is the empirical search, unenlightened by theory and explanation—a search for a needle in a haystack. Whereas the second approach can lead to profitable trading models, there is often little understanding of why the model works.

A simple example of this approach would proceed as follows. A trader is dabbling with a program that lets him get profit and loss figures on any system he enters into the program. He tinkers with a formula that he found in a book which struck his fancy. One or two of the 30 variations show marginal profit on one period of history in one market. The trader thinks this looks promising. He optimizes the model on one year of current data and finds great profit. He starts trading it on Monday. Real-time trading performance is poor. He keeps on trading until he loses half his equity and concludes that the trading system "fell apart." The trader starts looking through his library for any other system or formula that strikes his fancy.

To understand the results of a trading model, seven steps must be followed to build and test it:

1. Formulate the trading strategy.
2. Write the rules in a definitive form.
3. Test the trading strategy.
4. Optimize the trading strategy.
5. Trade the strategy.
6. Monitor trading performance and compare it to test performance.
7. Improve and refine the trading strategy.

Each of these steps depends on the success of the preceding one (see Figure 2–1). Continuous feedback, using information from later steps to

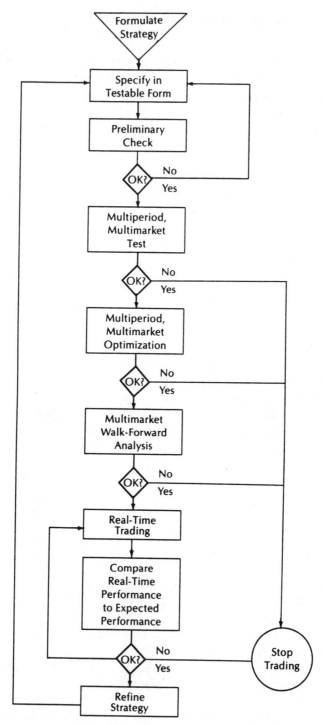

Figure 2-1 The Path to Knowledge

go back and improve earlier steps, is an essential component of this approach and one of its great strengths. With a good system, the approach leads to a continuous evolution, refinement, and improvement of the trading strategy.

STEP 1: FORMULATE THE TRADING STRATEGY

A trading system begins as an idea. The rules that constitute the strategy must be laid out one at a time. The strategy can be as simple or complex as desired. The simplicity or complexity of the strategy ultimately does not matter. What does matter is that the strategy be spelled out completely and consistently.

For example, go long when the market rallies more than 125% of yesterday's daily range from the close. Go short when the market falls the same amount. Exit positions on opposite entry signals.

Incomplete specification of all the rules of the strategy is one of the most common mistakes in system development. This is especially true for traders new to system development.

The two minimum requirements for a trading strategy are a rule to enter the market and a rule to exit the market. Typically, a strategy consists of buy and sell conditions that "mirror" each other. For example, a buy signal occurs when the price rises through a 3-day high and a sell signal occurs when the price breaks through a 3-day low. This is a *symmetrical trading system*.

A strategy can also consist of completely different buy-and-sell entry conditions. For example, a buy signal occurs when a 5-day high is broken, and a sell signal occurs when a 5-day moving average falls below a 20-day moving average. This is an *asymmetrical trading system*.

Typically, a trading strategy includes *risk management,* which is a way to limit the amount of capital at risk when a position is first entered. A typical approach is to set a stop-loss order, which is the maximum loss to be taken on a trade. For example, assume that a long position is initiated at a price of 395.00 in the Standard and Poor's (S&P) 500 futures contract. The strategy calls for a maximum risk of $1,000, or 2.00 points, at trade entry. Therefore, a sell stop is also entered along with the position. If $1,000 = 2.00 points, then the sell stop is 395.00 − 2.00 points, or 393.00.

A trading strategy can also include *profit management,* which protects the open equity profit that develops during the life of the position. A typical profit management approach for a long position is to set a trailing stop at a fixed dollar amount from the equity high, that is, the highest close achieved during the life of the trade. Assume a strategy that calls for a trailing stop $2,000, or 4.00 S&P points, under the equity high close of a long position. Assume that the long position is entered at a price of 390.00 and an equity high point of 398.00 is reached on the fourth day of the position. A sell stop is entered at 394.00 (398.00 − 4.00 points = 394.00). This locks in $2,000 in profit (394.00 − 390.00 = 4 points × $500 per point = $2,000).

Another variation of profit management is the *leading target order.* It is a more aggressive way of seizing a profit that occurs during the life of the trade. A typical target approach is to set an *or better* order at a fixed dollar amount above or below the position price. Assume a strategy that calls for an *or better* order $2,000, or 4.00 points, above a long position. A long position is initiated in the S&P at a price of 375.00. An order is entered to *sell at 379.00 or better* (375.00 + 4.00 points = 379.00). This approach will effectively take a $2,000, or 4.00-point profit the moment the market reaches this price during the life of the trade.

STEP 2: WRITE THE RULES IN A DEFINITIVE FORM

The following example takes a "vague" strategy and transforms it into a precise, well-formulated, testable strategy. Joe Trader uses a trading strategy that employs moving averages in a quasi-systematic manner. He has enjoyed some degree of success employing these common yet useful indicators in a particular way. He believes he could do a lot better if he knew more about them. He therefore went out and hired Alex Programmer to write a computer program that will allow him precisely to formulate and test this trading strategy. The following conversation ensued at their first meeting, as Joe explained his method:

JOE: I buy them when the moving averages look good and I sell them when the averages look bad.
ALEX: Hmm, that's pretty interesting. Does it work?
JOE: Sometimes.
ALEX: Interesting. But we are going to need to be a little more specific to get this thing off the ground. Do you mind if I ask you a few questions?

JOE: I guess not, but I hope it won't take too long. I have got to make some money. I want to take the family to Europe this summer. Let's get going.

ALEX: OK. Let us start with the buy part. Can you first tell me what you mean by the averages looking good?

JOE: Ya, but I think it's pretty obvious. The averages look good when the short one just blasts through the long one.

ALEX: Well it may be obvious to you, but not to me. By "blasts through" do you mean that average one crosses from under to over average two?

JOE: Ya.

ALEX: Good. Does it matter how much average one crosses over average two?

JOE: Sometimes yes, sometimes no. It all depends.

ALEX: On what?

JOE: It's hard to say.

ALEX: Well then maybe we should leave how much it crosses over for future improvements. Let's just get the basic system going. We know that we will go long the market if average one crosses from under to over average two. Now what do you mean by "the averages look bad"?

JOE: That should be obvious too. They just fall apart, go to hell in a handcart.

ALEX: Well, since we go long when average one comes from under to over average two, am I correct in assuming that we go short when average one crosses from over to under average two?

JOE: Ya, you got it, champ.

ALEX: Good. This looks like we are always in a position. Is that correct?

JOE: Most of the time.

ALEX: When are you not in a position?

JOE: When the whole thing just falls apart.

ALEX: What do you mean by that?

JOE: When the market isn't moving, moving averages just cut me to pieces.

ALEX: What do you mean when you say "the market isn't moving"?

JOE: There is just no action. Lots of little swings, but no big swings.

ALEX: Does that mean that this moving average strategy is really only able to catch big swings?

JOE: Ya.

ALEX: What is a big swing then?

JOE: That depends.

ALEX: On what?

JOE: The market.

ALEX: I see. Does this vary from market to market and from year to year?

JOE: You got it.

ALEX: Do different length moving averages have an impact on this?

JOE: Ya.

ALEX: How do you determine which ones to use?

JOE: I play around with different moving averages in my charting program and use the ones that look pretty good.

ALEX: Well, you don't know anything about the profit and risk performance of these averages that "look pretty good," do you?

JOE: No, I don't. That's why I hired you. You're supposed to figure this all out for me.

ALEX: Well, I will do my best. How do you control your risk when you take a position?

JOE: It depends. If one average just blows through the other like a bat out of hell, I usually make some money right away and it's no problem. But sometimes the market just looks pretty lame and I put in a close stop on the position.

ALEX: You mean sometimes you use a stop and sometimes you don't?

JOE: Ya.

ALEX: That sounds inconsistent and could be dangerous as well. Do you want to test the strategy with and without a risk stop?

JOE: Ya.

ALEX: OK. I will build this in as an option. What do you do when you have a winner?

JOE: If I get a couple of grand in it, I usually ring the cash register.

ALEX: Do you mean that you take a profit after you have made a certain amount of money in position?

JOE: Ya.

ALEX: How much is enough?

JOE: It depends.

ALEX: On what?

JOE: The market. How I have been doing lately. How I feel. A lot of stuff.

ALEX: Well, should I build in some kind of profit idea as an option in the program?

JOE: Ya.

ALEX: Let us see what we have got here. Our basic trading model uses two different length moving averages. The model is always either long or short. We go long if the short average goes from under to over the longer average. We go short when the short average goes from above to below the longer average. Is that right so far?

JOE: So far so good.

ALEX: There are two variations on this basic model. A risk stop and a target order. The use of either of these will lead to a fundamental alteration of the model. If a position is exited using a risk stop or a profit or better target order, then the model will not always be in the market. Is that OK?

JOE: Let's just play it by ear and find out.

ALEX: OK. I will set up this program to have user-definable moving average lengths. It will be an option to use a risk stop or a target profit or better. The program will be capable of testing a batch of different length moving average combinations. Do you think this will do it?

JOE: It's a start. Let's see what happens.

This little melodrama serves to highlight the vagueness that will surround an incomplete trading idea. Although Joe Trader may seem excessive, he is more reality than fiction. And Alex Programmer was a lot better communicator and more accommodating than many a programmer. Furthermore, this dialogue went a lot smoother than most such conversations.

In its final form, a trading system is a set of precise rules and formulas. If the trading idea cannot be reduced to such, it is not a trading system. The trading system discussed in the preceding dialogue can be described in three ways: ordinary English, precise rules and formula, and computer code.

In English, this moving average trading system can be expressed as the following list of rules:

Rule 1. Go long when the short-term moving average crosses above the long-term moving average.

Rule 2. Once long, stay long until a sell entry occurs.

Rule 3. Go short when the short-term moving average crosses below the long-term moving average.

Rule 4. Once short, stay short until a buy entry occurs.

The trading system can be defined as the following set of formulas and rules:

Definition 1: $C(t)$ is the close of the tth day with $t = 1$ the present day.

Definition 2: x is the length of moving average one (MA1).

Definition 3: y is the length of moving average two (MA2).

Formula 1: $\text{MA1} = [C(t) + C(t + 1) + \ldots + C(t + x - 1)]/x$

Formula 2: $MA2 = [C(t) + C(t+1) + \ldots + C(t+y-1)]/y$

Rule 1: y is never less than 2 times x.

Rule 2: If $MA1(t) > MA2(t)$ and $MA1(t-1) < MA2(t-1)$, then go long.

Rule 3: If long and $MA1(t) > MA2(t)$ then do nothing.

Rule 4: If $MA1(t) < MA2(t)$ and $MA1(t-1) > MA2(t-1)$, then go short.

Rule 5: If short and $MA1(t) < MA2(t)$, then do nothing.

Such ideas look quite a bit different in the "C" programming language. The "C" code to calculate the value of a moving average is displayed below:

```
int SMA(int day,int period,int type,float *value)

{

        register int i;
        float total;

        *value = 0.0;

        if (period<=0)
                period = 1;

        if (day < period)
                return(-1);

        total = 0.0;

        for (i = 0; i<period; i++)
                total += get_price_data( type, day-i);

        *value = total/(float) period;

        return(1);
```

By comparison, the final version of this trading system in "C" takes care of every last detail and is 8,187 lines long. It is more accurate than the English description. In this form, it can be tested precisely against price data.

User-friendly software programs have been specifically designed for the nonprogramming trader who is not proficient in "C" or some other programming language.[1] These programs allow the trader to describe and test trading ideas without the proficiency of a programmer. This is not to say that proper results can be expected from an incorrectly specified system. However, these programs do have a number of built-in functions and operations that make the specification of a trading system a great deal easier.

Examples in this book will use *Advanced Trader;* however, other available programs must give the user the same abilities to express rules

---

[1] The author is the developer of *Advanced Trader,* one of the leading programs available.

definitively, and to test and optimize these rules. A trading idea is expressed in a Script, which is the trading and testing language of *Advanced Trader*. A Script that expresses the preceding specified two moving-average trading system looks like this:

```
Period__1 = 5

MA1__Today = sma[c:,Period__1,0,0]

MA1__Yesterday = sma[c:, Period__1,0,1]

Period__2 = 20

MA2__Today = sma[c:,Period__2,0,0]

MA2__Yesterday = sma[c:,Period__2,0,1]

Longif MA1__Today > MA2__Today then

        Longif MA1__Yesterday < MA2__Yesterday then

            Order #1

                    buy net__position + 1 at MOO

            end__order

        Endif

Endif

Longif MA1__Today < MA2__Today then

    Longif MA1__Yesterday > MA2__Yesterday then

            Order #2

                    sell net__position + 1 at MOO

            end__order

        Endif

    Endif
```

As you can see, this Script is a lot easier to understand than the "C" code. It is a little more condensed than the English version and it looks a lot like the definition and formula version. The Script defines "Period—1" as the number "5" and "Period—2" as 20. It further defines "MA1—Today" as a simple moving average of length 5 for the current day (i.e., **sma [c:,Period—1,0,0]**), and so on for other values of the moving average on close prices.

The *buy* condition is set in what is called a "longif" statement. A longif statement is a way of using a condition—that is, if this is true, then do this; if it is false, do something else. When these conditions are met, an order is set to buy and reverse the current short position with a market-on-open order the next day (**MOO**). The sell condition is also set in a different "longif" statement. When these conditions are met, an order is set to sell and reverse the current long position with a market-on-open order the next day (**MOO**).

This Script will do the exact same thing as the "C" code with a lot less effort and in a lot less time because of all the built-in features of *Advanced Trader*. Some of these key features include data management, trading management, and hundreds of built-in functions that are useful in trading.

STEP 3: TEST THE TRADING STRATEGY

The trading system is now in a form that can be tested. The testing stage has two goals. The first goal is to determine if the trading system is doing what it was told. In other words, is it buying when the short moving average crosses above the long moving average and selling when the short moving average crosses below the long moving average? To determine this, a single test of the trading system is run on one piece of price data. The trading signals are then "hand checked" on a day-by-day basis. If the system is functioning correctly, this completes the first stage of testing. If it is not, it must be fixed and retested.

The second goal is to get a rough idea of the profit-and-risk profile of this system prior to optimization. The model should be moderately profitable over a number of markets and over a number of different time periods. Every test does not have to be a winner; however, if every test is a loser, the system should be abandoned. In general, initial results with reasonable parameters should justify your confidence.

This level of testing is not intended to be either exhaustive or definitive. It is rather a panoramic view of performance based on "reasonable" parameter values over a number of markets and over a number of time periods.

To accomplish the second level of testing, the simple moving-average crossover system will be tested on the markets and data shown in Figure 2–2.

This test includes a mix of both markets and time periods. This test batch consists of 24 different tests, 5 different markets, and a 10-year time span viewed in 2-year cross sections. The system will be tested with parameters of 5- and 40-day moving averages. The results of the 24 tests are summarized in Figure 2–3.

What should be expected from such a test? Not too much, really. If every test is very profitable (e.g., greater than $10,000), a winning system has been found. Of course, this assumes that all aspects of testing are correct and the simulations are realistic. However, if every test is a big loser

	1981–82	1983–84	1985–86	1987–88	1989–90	Number of Tests
Cattle	x	x	x	x	x	5
Soybeans	x	x	x	x	x	5
S&P 500		x	x	x	x	4
S-Francs	x	x	x	x	x	5
T-Bonds	x	x	x	x	x	5

Figure 2-2 Markets and Data

(e.g., losing more than $10,000 a year), it is just as clearly a worthless system. (There are some subtle exceptions to this rule of thumb; they will be discussed, in later chapters.) In all likelihood, this system should be abandoned at this stage. If, as is likely, the results are mixed (i.e., a few big wins and some big losses, along with a mix of smaller wins and losses), it is acceptable to go on to the optimization stage. Continue with the next stage of system development except when the majority of tests are large losses.

STEP 4: OPTIMIZE THE TRADING SYSTEM

Now that the system has satisfactorily passed the first series of tests, it is time to go on to the next step: optimization. The following definition appears in the *American Heritage Dictionary*[2]: **Optimize:** *To make the most effective use of.*

As this definition indicates, to *optimize* a trading system is to make the most effective use of it. This is the true purpose of trading system optimization. Unfortunately, a long history of abuse has caused the word to be falsely confused with the term *curve-fitting.*

Curve-fitting, which means to approximate a line to a body of data, is also widely misunderstood and is often incorrectly taken as a synonym for the term *overfitting.* Overfitting occurs when excessive attention is paid to creating a curve or testing a trading model with past data and not enough attention is paid to judging the predictive value of the curve or the trading model. Chapter 9 will expand the subject of overfitting.

Optimization has many pitfalls. This book is designed to point them out and thereby to help avoid them. The correct use of testing and optimization will extract the most understanding and profit from a trading

---

[2] *American Heritage Dictionary,* Houghton Mifflin Co., Boston.

Future	P & L	Drawdown	# Trades	% Wins
Cattle				
1981–82	($ 560)	$ 3,180	16	25%
1983–84	($ 1,364)	$ 4,844	17	17%
1985–86	$ 6,672	$ 2,640	11	54%
1987–88	$ 1,500	$ 3,648	11	45%
1989–90	($ 1,244)	$ 2,040	17	29%
Averages	$ 1,001	$ 3,270	14	34%
Soybeans				
1981–82	$10,350	$ 1,950	11	54%
1983–84	$18,512	$ 3,925	13	46%
1985–86	($ 7,300)	$ 7,387	23	30%
1987–88	$11,375	$ 5,075	12	50%
1989–90	($ 9,662)	$ 9,662	15	20%
Averages	$ 4,655	$ 5,600	24	40%
S&P 500				
1981–82				
1983–84	($22,250)	$22,250	23	13%
1985–86	($ 7,425)	$23,050	14	42%
1987–88	$14,375	$19,425	17	29%
1989–90	($ 8,225)	$35,350	18	33%
Averages	($ 5,881)	$25,019	18	29%
Swiss Francs				
1981–82	$ 2,787	$ 3,875	16	43%
1983–84	$ 8,362	$ 1,800	13	53%
1985–86	($13,350)	$13,350	20	20%
1987–88	$11,325	$ 7,925	16	37%
1989–90	$14,187	$ 3,775	14	42%
Averages	$ 4,662	$ 6,145	15	39%
Treasury Bonds				
1981–82	$ 2,693	$ 8,981	14	28%
1983–84	($ 4,268)	$10,056	13	15%
1985–86	$27,456	$ 6,362	12	41%
1987–88	$ 5,312	$ 4,981	15	33%
1989–90	($ 3,287)	$ 8,500	16	25%
Averages	$ 5,581	$ 7,776	14	28%

Figure 2-3   The Results of the Test

system. The basic idea of optimization is simple to understand. But it is nearly impossible to do correctly without a full understanding of all of the principles involved.

In a practical sense, optimization is the process of calculating the performance of a large number of different tests of the trading system on the same piece of price data. Tests vary from each other because each test applies a different set of the model variable values that are "under optimization" (i.e., the subject of the test). A small set of top models are selected from this large group of different test results based on a predefined set of evaluation parameters. If the optimization and the selection process were both done with the proper attention to all the appropriate rules, the top models will be those that offer the greatest potential to profit in actual trading.

An Example of a Simple Optimization

The two moving-average crossover system is a good example of a simple optimization design. The trading model generates buy and sell signals when the two moving averages cross. The two candidates for optimization are the lengths, or periods, of the two moving averages. Since the two moving averages measure two different rates of trend, their length, or periods, should not be similar in length. Keeping this is mind, the variables will be optimized over the following ranges:

MA1 from 1 to 10 in steps of 1, or,

| 1 | 2 | 3 | 4 | 5 | 6 | 7 | 8 | 9 | 10 |

MA2 from 15 to 60 in steps of 5, or,

| 15 | 20 | 25 | 30 | 35 | 40 | 45 | 50 | 55 | 60 |

This example selects short values for the first moving average to focus on short trends and longer values for the second moving average to focus on long trends. Now what will actually happen during this optimization process?

The computer will sequence through each possible value of the first moving average starting with the first possible value for the second moving average. The first 10 tests will use the following combinations of moving averages:

| MA1 | 1 | 2 | 3 | 4 | 5 | 6 | 7 | 8 | 9 | 10 |
| MA2 | 15 | 15 | 15 | 15 | 15 | 15 | 15 | 15 | 15 | 15 |

After all available values of Variable 1 (1 through 10) have been tested against the first value of Variable 2 (15), this process will then be repeated with the second value of Variable 2. In other words, values from 1 through 10 for the short moving average are next tested against a value of 20 for the long moving average.

MA1	1	2	3	4	5	6	7	8	9	10
MA2	20	20	20	20	20	20	20	20	20	20

This process is repeated until all combinations of variables for both moving averages are calculated and evaluated. In this particular optimization, there are 100 (10 for Variable 1 × 10 for Variable 2 = 100 tests) variable combinations.

The trading model is evaluated based on its trading performance with each combination of variables. The computer calculates the net profit and loss and a number of other trading statistics for the trading model with a 1-day moving average and a 10-day moving average. These statistics are stored and will be compared with the statistics of all other variable combinations. A set of "top models" will be selected from the trading statistics of the 100 different variations of the moving average trading system.

A broad improvement of profit performance is expected over that which was found during the first level of testing. For example, a very good test would show at least a 25% overall improvement in profit, a reduction of drawdown, an increase in the number of profitable systems, and an increase in the percentage of winning trades from those found in the first series of tests.

The Walk-Forward Analysis

If the optimization shows improved performance, it is time to go on to the final step in the testing process: the *walk-forward analysis*. The walk-forward analysis judges the performance of a trading system strictly on the basis of postoptimization or out-of-sample trading. The walk-forward analysis is the closest simulation possible of the way in which an optimizable trading system is used in real time. This level of testing answers three essential questions for trading a system with intelligence and confidence:

1. Will the trading model make money after optimization?
2. At what rate will the trading model make money after optimization?
3. How will changes in trend, volatility, and liquidity affect trading performance?

The walk-forward analysis is discussed in detail in Chapter 7, "Optimizing the Trading System."

The first and most important benefit of the walk-forward analysis is the verification of the forward-trading ability of the model. In other words, does the model have life after optimization? Will it make money in real time? Of course, the walk-forward test is not real-time trading, but it is a much more realistic simulation.

Overfitting is defined and discussed in detail in Chapter 9, "The Many Faces of Overfitting." At this point, note that overfitting is the process of applying too many rules or variables, or manipulating the data. It is a mistake that can occur in many ways. In effect, overfitting too closely "fits" the variables of the trading system to the data on which the system is being tested. The reason this is harmful is that the model is being fit to random or nonpredictive aspects of price movement. The symptoms of overfitting are clear: great results during optimization, and poor results during trading.

Evidence has accumulated that shows two simple but striking truths about overfitting. An overfit or improperly tested trading model has a high likelihood of losing money. However, a poor trading system can show profit somewhere during optimization based on overfitting. However, it is even more shocking to note that a good trading idea can lose money in real time if it has been overfit or improperly optimized. Walk-forward analysis detects this and is one of its great benefits.

The walk-forward analysis adds a very important step to the traditional optimization procedure. It tests the performance of the model variables on data that were not included in the optimization. This is also known as *out-of-sample testing* and as *forward testing.*

It is a certainty that a poor or overfit strategy will not make money in a walk-forward analysis. In all probability, even a good model that is overfit will not make money in a walk-forward analysis. However, the only way to find this out is by testing.

Studies have shown that a randomly chosen, poor or overfit model can make money in one or two walk-forward tests. Studies have also shown, however, that such a model will not make money over a large number of walk-forward tests. Therefore, to achieve the greatest confidence, a series of walk-forward tests, or a *walk-forward analysis*, must be performed on a trading model. A trading model that makes a significant overall profit in a large number of walk-forward tests, where at least 50% of the tests are profitable, is likely to be successful.

The second benefit of the walk-forward analysis is a more precise and reliable measure of the rates of postoptimization profit and risk. This is also explained in more detail in Chapter 7. A walk-forward analysis produces a statistical profile of multiple optimizations and postoptimization trading periods. This offers greater statistical validity than the traditional optimization because it is based on a much larger sample. It makes possible a precise comparison and measurement of the rates of walk-forward trading profit versus optimization trading profit.

If a model is only making 25% of optimization profit in walk-forward trading, it is not achieving expectations. A properly fit model should perform at levels similar to those achieved during optimization. If a good model is performing at a rate much lower than that found in testing, in all likelihood it is too closely fit. If after further testing, this low performance threshold cannot be crossed, the conclusion must be that this is just not a good model.

The third benefit offered by the walk-forward analysis is insight into the impact of trend, volatility, and liquidity changes on trading performance. Research has shown that trend changes, which by nature occur swiftly, and large shifts in both volatility and liquidity can have a large and often negative impact on trading performance. A good, robust model will be more capable of "toughing out" or responding profitably to such changes.

The walk-forward analysis, rolling as it does over large segments of time viewed through cross sections, offers a lot of information regarding the impact of such market changes on trading performance. The user can easily isolate and assess the positive or negative impacts of unusual, nonrecurring events such as the stock market crash of 1987 or the Persian Gulf War.

An Example of a Simple Walk Forward

What would a simple walk-forward test look like? To construct such a test for a model, assume that the ideal optimization window is 4 years and the ideal walk-forward or trading window is 6 months. Twelve tests of the system should be sufficient. This test requires $9^{1}/_{2}$ years of price data.

The candidate for this example is S&P futures from 7/1/82 through 1/20/92. The walk-forward test will trade for $5^{1}/_{2}$ years from 7/1/86 through 1/20/92 in twelve 6-month postoptimization, walk-forward tests. Two variable ranges will be scanned:

Buy breakout percentage   0 to 750 in steps of 50
Sell breakout percentage   0 to 750 in steps of 50

The first step in the walk-forward test is an optimization of these two variables on the first 4-year optimization window of price data: 7/2/82 to 6/30/86. When this step is done, the result is a top model and its model values. These optimal values are then tested on the first 6-month trading window of price data: 7/1/86 to 12/31/86. To see how the model performed in the first walk-forward test, the net profit and loss of the top model in both the optimization and trading windows are evaluated and recorded.

Consider an example: Optimize the model on the first optimization window and find that the top model uses breakout values of 50% and 100% and produces a $36,670 net profit in 1982–1986. This top model is then tested on the last 6 months of 1986, and it generates a loss of $1,135. This is the walk-forward result. The process is then repeated on the next 48-month test window, 1/83–12/86. In turn, when the top model is found for this window, it is again tested on the next 6-month test window, 1/87–6/87. This process is repeated until all 12 optimization and walk-forward tests are completed. The last optimization window will be 1/88–12/91 and the last test window will be 1/92.

The walk-forward analysis records the results of these 12 optimizations, displayed in Figure 2–4, and totals the twelve walk-forward results, displayed in Figure 2–5. It also calculates and compares annualized rates of return for the optimization and walk-forward results. This statistic is

```
Blast v1.05.0X / Walk Forward Performance Summary / Date: Wednesday January 22, 1992          Page 3 of 20
-----------------------------------------------------------------------------------------------------------
Rollover Start  : S&P INDEX          D 03/88  07/01/82  End : S&P 500 Composite   D 03/92  01/20/92  Rollover Factor : -10

TOP MODEL #1 / ESTIMATION WINDOW SUMMARY / Analysis Days : 12132
-----------------------------------------------------------------------------------------------------------
              :  Net    :  Max    :  Open  :Number! Percent : AveWin/ ! Average :        ! Model   : Ave Win / !
Window        !Profit/Loss! Drawdown !  Equity !Trades!  Win   ! AveLoss : Trade   ! PROM !Efficiency! Ave Urg !
-----------------------------------------------------------------------------------------------------------
07/01/82 - 06/30/86 !  36670.00! -8855.00!   0.00!  275 !  40 X !  1.98!  133.3!  51.0!  1.92 X !  52.97 X !
01/03/83 - 12/31/86 !  14355.00! -7080.00!   0.00!   85 !  34 X !  2.34!  168.9!  -33.4!  0.75 X !  49.49 X !
07/01/83 - 06/30/87 !  71565.00! -8835.00!   0.00!  265 !  41 X !  2.18!  270.1!  168.2!  3.74 X !  55.30 X !
01/02/84 - 12/31/87 ! 116310.00! -11635.00!   0.00!  260 !  42 X !  2.39!  447.3!  321.5!  6.08 X !  53.34 X !
07/02/84 - 06/30/88 ! 133110.00! -11635.00!   0.00!  257 !  45 X !  2.27!  517.9!  385.6!  6.96 X !  51.82 X !
01/01/85 - 12/30/88 ! 132055.00! -11635.00!   0.00!  256 !  44 X !  2.25!  515.8!  377.7!  6.90 X !  51.48 X !
07/01/85 - 06/30/89 ! 130510.00! -11635.00!   0.00!  267 !  46 X !  2.03!  488.8!  352.3!  6.82 X !  51.30 X !
01/01/86 - 12/29/89 ! 149645.00! -11635.00!   0.00!  266 !  46 X !  2.02!  562.6!  419.6!  7.82 X !  51.70 X !
07/01/86 - 06/29/90 ! 141840.00! -11635.00!   0.00!  274 !  45 X !  2.00!  517.7!  381.4!  7.42 X !  51.45 X !
01/01/87 - 12/31/90 ! 172310.00! -11635.00!   0.00!  270 !  48 X !  1.95!  638.2!  501.4!  9.01 X !  50.70 X !
07/01/87 - 06/28/91 ! 139855.00! -15180.00!   0.00!  188 !  41 X !  2.53!  743.9!  365.7!  7.31 X !  54.35 X !
01/01/88 - 12/31/91 ! 124250.00! -18815.00!   0.00!  180 !  42 X !  2.36!  690.3!  314.3!  6.50 X !  55.63 X !
- - - - - - - - - !- - - - - -!- - - -!- - - -!- - - !- - - -!- - - -!- - - -!- - -!- - - - -!- - - - -!
TOTAL         : 1362475.00!         !   0.00! 2843 !       !        !        !       !        !          !
- - - - - - - - - !- - - - - -!- - - -!- - - -!- - - !- - - -!- - - -!- - - -!- - -!- - - - -!- - - - -!
LARGEST       :  172310.00! -18815.00!   0.00!  275 !  48 X !  2.53!  743.9!  501.4!  9.01 X !  55.63 X !
SMALLEST      :   14355.00! -7080.00!   0.00!   85 !  34 X !  1.88!  133.3!  -33.4!  0.75 X !  49.49 X !
AVERAGE       :  113539.59! -11684.17!   0.00!  236 !  43 X !  2.18!  474.6!  300.4!  5.94 X !  52.46 X !
ANNUALIZED NET P&L !  29648.32!
-----------------------------------------------------------------------------------------------------------
```

Figure 2–4   Estimation Window Summary

```
Blast v1.05.0X / Walk Forward Performance Summary / Date: Wednesday January 22, 1992        Page 5 of 20
----------------------------------------------------------------------------------------------------
Rollover Start : S&P INDEX        D 03/88  07/01/82  End : S&P 500 Composite  D 03/92  01/20/92  Rollover Factor : -10

TOP MODEL #1 / NET PROFIT AND LOSS SUMMARY / Analysis Days : 1403
----------------------------------------------------------------------------------------------------
```

Window	Net Profit/Loss	Max Drawdown	Open Equity	Number Trades	Percent Win	AveWin/AveLoss	Average Trade	PROM	Model Efficiency	Ave Win / Ave Urg
07/01/86 - 12/31/86	-1135.00	-8835.00	0.00	40	32 %	2.00	-28.4	-54.1	-0.06 %	55.57 %
01/01/87 - 06/30/87	30675.00	-2920.00	0.00	8	50 %	10.72	3834.4	48.7	1.60 %	64.02 %
07/01/87 - 12/31/87	53390.00	-11635.00	0.00	30	53 %	2.81	1779.7	115.3	2.79 %	49.94 %
01/01/88 - 06/30/88	15220.00	-7530.00	0.00	33	54 %	1.47	461.2	13.6	0.80 %	41.56 %
07/01/88 - 12/30/88	-4040.00	-5795.00	0.00	40	35 %	1.58	-101.0	-56.3	-0.21 %	47.86 %
01/02/89 - 06/30/89	4360.00	-11200.00	0.00	37	45 %	1.37	117.8	-33.5	0.23 %	52.77 %
07/03/89 - 12/29/89	14370.00	-6910.00	0.00	38	44 %	1.77	378.2	-12.3	0.75 %	55.02 %
01/01/90 - 06/29/90	21760.00	-6165.00	0.00	37	51 %	1.77	588.1	25.2	1.14 %	54.63 %
07/02/90 - 12/31/90	29415.00	-9840.00	0.00	34	50 %	2.00	865.1	34.4	1.54 %	51.79 %
01/01/91 - 06/28/91	-18795.00	-24265.00	0.00	39	28 %	1.59	-481.9	-144.6	-0.98 %	47.09 %
07/01/91 - 12/31/91	37335.00	-1960.00	0.00	16	68 %	3.67	2333.4	94.4	1.95 %	60.20 %
01/01/92 - 01/20/92	100.00	0.00	0.00	1	100 %	100.00	100.0	0.0	0.01 %	3.54 %
TOTAL	182655.00		0.00	353						
LARGEST	53390.00	-24265.00	0.00	40	100 %	100.00	3834.4	115.3	2.79 %	64.02 %
SMALLEST	-18795.00	0.00	0.00	1	28 %	1.37	-481.9	-144.6	-0.98 %	3.54 %
AVERAGE	15221.25	-8079.58	0.00	29	51 %	10.89	820.6	2.6	0.80 %	48.66 %
ANNUALIZED NET P&L	34369.86									
WF EFFICIENCY	115.93									

Figure 2-5   Net Profit and Loss Summary

walk-forward efficiency. As a general rule, a walk-forward efficiency of 50% or more is considered one measure of a successful walk-forward analysis. Figure 2-5 displays a walk-forward efficiency of 115.93%.

A trading system passes a walk-forward analysis if it performs with overall profitability, shows a walk-forward efficiency of 50% or better, and has 50% or more of profitable walk-forward tests. If this is the case, the performance of the system must now be thoroughly analyzed. This is covered in detail in Chapter 7.

A primary consideration is the distribution of profit, loss, and trades. The more even the distribution of these elements over the entire span of the walk-forward analysis, the better. A walk-forward analysis can be invalidated by any unusually large win, winning run, or winning time period that contributes more than 50% of net profit. If the trading system satisfies the necessary criteria, then it is time to begin trading.

STEP 5: TRADE THE SYSTEM

Trading the system, after it has been exhaustively tested and evaluated, is the easy part. The signals and stops must be generated on a day-by-day basis exactly in accordance with the formula and rules that were evaluated in the testing process.

To assure the highest likelihood of success, all signals from the system must be taken without exception. Larry Williams, a notable trading system guru has said: *Trading systems work. System traders do not.*

In other words, profitable trading systems exist. Profitable system traders are rare. Many traders lack sufficient confidence in and understanding of their trading systems to stick with them when they begin their inevitable periods of drawdown. Many traders also lack the self-discipline required to stick rigorously with a mechanical trading system.

Experience indicates that systematic trading is one of the best ways to make money. The reason is consistency in entries and in exits and, more importantly, in trading risk and profit. Consistency alone will not assure profit; however, without consistent entries, exits, and risk, profit and risk cannot be managed. Without the management of risk, there is little chance of profit.

The lesson is simple. When a trading system has been satisfactorily tested and is performing in real-time trading according to expectation, stick with it and take every signal. This is not to say that a trading system will not have losing streaks. They will. It is the job of the trader to understand exactly what type of risk and drawdown are typical of the trading system. It is also the job of the trader to have adequate capitalization for these drawdowns in order to realize the profits to follow.

The trader should never blindly follow a trading system that has gotten off track. The best and most exhaustively tested trading systems can run into trouble, often as the result of markets changing character. A dramatic contraction of market volume and volatility can lead to a lack of liquidity and price movement. Most systems will do poorly in such conditions. Conversely, some markets manifest highly erratic and unprecedented volatility. This can prove damaging to trading systems. If these conditions represent only a small part of the tested data, then it is likely that the system will not do well—but only for a short time.

Remember, all trading systems are tested on past price behavior. If a trading system runs into price behavior that is highly antithetical to it, or that it has never before "seen," it may well run into losses. Most often, this period will not last long; but when trading a system, it is imperative to know at what point to abandon it. This is determined by the system stop loss defined and discussed in Chapter 10, "The Evaluation of Real-Time Trading."

A thorough understanding of the performance of the trading system, its profit and risk profile, and the system stop loss will generate the confidence required to take every signal offered by the system. This confidence and a thoroughly tested, profitable trading system are what it takes to be a good system trader.

STEP 6: COMPARE TEST WITH TRADE PROFITS

To trade a system successfully, the user must closely monitor its real-time performance. It is essential to understand that a properly designed and tested trading system should continue to behave the same way in real-time trading as it did during testing. Conditions arise that can alter this equilibrium. However, it is essential that if they do, the trader understand the cause of the deviation.

Many traders are too quick to abandon a trading system when it is losing, although the rate and size of losses may be typical of the system. The reasons are usually ignorance of and lack of confidence in the trading system.

Yet few traders are alarmed when a system starts profiting at a pace that is better than expectation. This serious deviation, albeit a far more pleasant one, must also be explained. Understanding why this is happening may provide important information.

Such knowledge may help anticipate future pleasant surprises. It may also point to the probability of larger losses since larger than expected profits are usually a result of growing volatility, and the flip side of rising volatility is often larger losses. This knowledge can also lead to improvements in the trading system.

It is important to track and tabulate the real-time performance of the trading system. This real-time trading profit and loss must be continually compared with the test profit and loss of the system. Both test and real-time performance profiles must be maintained. These performance profiles monitor the essential statistics that define performance. Some of the key elements are:

1. The frequency and duration of trading.
2. The maximum drawdown.
3. The maximum run-up.
4. The size and length of the average losing trade.
5. The number of trades, duration, and dollar amount of the average losing run.
6. The size and length of the average winning trade.
7. The number of trades, duration, and dollar value of the average winning run.

Armed with this information, the evaluation of real-time performance becomes mechanical. Any deviation of real-time performance from test performance either must be satisfactorily explained or trading the system must be stopped.

Reasons for System Failure

Consider the worst case scenario: Losses occur in excess of the system stop loss and a trading is terminated. It was decided in advance that if the maximum losing run found in testing was exceeded by 50% in real-time trading without a counterbalancing improvement in the rate of profit, then real-time trading of the system would stop. There are three possible causes:

1. It is a poor system that escaped the test checks and balances.
2. It is a good system that was improperly optimized.
3. Unusually adverse or untested market conditions emerged.

If all the testing steps outlined in this chapter were followed, it is quite unlikely that the system is just poor. However, if the system was tested carelessly, it is possible. If this is found to be the case, then test the trading system properly.

In a similar fashion, if the test procedures outlined in this chapter were followed carefully and without bias, the second cause is also unlikely. However, if you have reason to believe that the strategy is sound, then it is worth rechecking your work, paying particular attention to the details of each trade looking for errors in logic.

With a well-designed and thoroughly tested system, the third cause of failure is most likely. As was mentioned earlier in this section, dramatic changes in volume, liquidity, size and frequency of gaps, volatility, and trend can wreak havoc with the best designed and tested systems.

However, a failure here is really a failure of testing. Markets by nature contain a variety of changing situations. It is necessary to test the trading system on a large enough sample of data to prevent such performance lapses. Markets do run hot and cold, and for this reason the sample must be broad. If a very active and good trading market simply "dries up," this can adversely impact a trading system. Performance of the trading system in such conditions must also be known.

For these reasons, it is critical to test a trading system on a highly diversified set of price data, including high volatility, low volatility, bull market, bear market, sideways market, congestion, and so on. Only in this way can you reduce the probability of running into real-time price action different from that on which your trading system has been tested. If a trading system has not been tested on a particular type of market or condition, its performance in such a circumstance cannot possibly be known. Incomplete testing based on such omissions will translate directly into trading losses.

If improper testing or optimization is not the cause of the system failure, look to an incomplete data sample as the likely cause. All these causes of failure can most likely be corrected by more careful crafting the second time around. However, keep in mind that a poor system is a poor system, and no amount of testing will make it a good system.

Poor Testing

Poor testing is easier to overcome. Just do it right. If it turns out that the system was good and was tested incorrectly, remember the high cost of such sloppy work. This should improve concentration the next time.

Adverse Conditions

If the cause of failure is adverse market action, there are two choices. Incorporate such data in the test sample and retest the system. If this proves impossible, wait out the adverse market condition and then begin trading again.

A Profitable Outcome

The second outcome of real-time trading is a more pleasant alternative: profit. However, do not let profit cause overconfidence or a drop in vigilance. Continue to monitor the system rigorously. Compare it regularly with its test profile. If it exceeds or falls below its test profile, the circumstances must be explained. If the rate of real-time profit changes, it must be evaluated. Remember, the markets are bigger than any trader. The trader who is caught off guard will soon be looking for a new profession.

Profits beyond expectation can signal a forthcoming problem. Although this time exceptional action was a benefit, the next time it could lead to proportionately higher losses. Large profits can be a "warning not heeded."

STEP 7: IMPROVING THE SYSTEM

A continual observation of the performance of the trading system on an entry-by-entry, trade-by-trade, and exit-by-exit basis can provide valuable information to the trader. Such close inspection is likely to suggest many ideas for improvement of the original trading logic over time. Of course, with each improvement, the entire development and testing process must be carefully reapplied.

3

TRADING SYSTEM STRUCTURE

A *trading system* is a mechanical means of trading systematically. The *American Heritage Dictionary* defines *system* as: *A set of interrelated ideas, principles, rules, procedures, laws or the like.*

The key words here are *interrelated* and *rules: A trading system is a set of interrelated rules to enter and exit a market.*

A trading system can be as simple as: *Buy when the coin flip is heads and sell when the flip is tails.*

It is essential for a trading system to be objective, consistent, and complete. The complexity of the trading rules has no limit. Nor is simplicity in a system necessarily a drawback.

There are thousands of trading systems. They come in all forms: moving-average crossovers, volatility breakouts, channels, single-day patterns, multiple-day patterns, chart patterns, indicator-based systems, and on and on.

WHY USE A TRADING SYSTEM?

The purpose of trading is to produce profits. The main reasons a trading system helps this pursuit are its quantifiability, verifiability, consistency, and objectivity.

Quantification

A properly tested trading system provides the quantitative measures necessary to make the decisions required to trade systematically, rationally, and profitably.

A computer-tested trading system quantifies profit and risk. It also produces a large number of other very useful statistics that provide insight into the internal operation of the trading system, and knowledge of what can be expected from it when it is traded.

As already mentioned, without a statistically reliable measurement of profit, it is impossible to anticipate future profits and losses. Without this, it is impossible to evaluate the quality of the return.

More importantly, without a statistically reliable measure of risk, it is impossible to manage risk. There is no profitable trading without risk management. Risk is what dictates how much it costs to trade a system. A portfolio management program cannot be designed until it is known what it costs to get the profit.

There can be no real assessment of the essential risk/reward features of a system without comparing profit with required risk. Consider two examples. In the first system, a profit of $2,500 per year is earned with a risk of $500. This is not a terribly profitable system. Yet neither is it a very risky one. Furthermore, it offers a reward-to-risk ratio of 5 to 1 ($2,500/$500 = 5). This makes the system very appealing.

The second system earns $50,000 profit a year with a risk of $50,000. This is a very profitable system, and an equally risky one. Its reward-to-risk ratio of 1 to 1 is very unappealing. Which system is better? Judging by profit alone, the second. Judging by what it costs to earn a dollar of profit, the first is worth five times more than the second. Profit and risk are inextricably interrelated.

Verification

Why must a trading system be verified? To see if it works. To see what the profit and risk of the system is over many types of different markets and ever-changing market conditions. Without this essential information, risk cannot be managed and informed trading cannot be done. This information is also required to calculate expectations, the cost of doing business, and the rate of profit.

An objectively formulated set of trading rules can be programmed into a computer. This programmed trading system can then be tested over years of price history and over many different stocks, futures, and options markets. A bunch of vague and inconsistent ideas cannot be tested and measured. They can be traded. Only a broker and an open account are required. The results of such activity, however, are well documented and predictable. They provide an assured entry into that nonexclusive 95%-of-all traders-who-trade-lose club.

Objectivity

The *American Heritage Dictionary* offers the following definition of *objective: Uninfluenced by emotion, surmise, or personal prejudice.* In other words, an *objective rule* is readily repeatable and is uninfluenced by those killers of all profit, whimsy and emotion. There is nothing wrong with emotion. It is essential to life. However, emotion as a trading input is usually quite unreliable. The same event is likely to elicit a different emotional response depending on whether the trader is healthy or sick, rested or exhausted, hungry or satisfied, happy or sad, tense or calm, and so on. Emotion is the enemy of consistency; objectivity is its ally. Objectivity also makes verification possible, the third major benefit of the trading system.

Consistency

Why is consistency so important to profit? Consistency is one of the major factors in risk control. When risk is defined, it can be measured, monitored, and controlled. It is impossible to control risk when it is undefined or changing. Without consistency of entry, exit, and risk on each and every trade, it is impossible to estimate the probability of success.

Consistency also means knowing in advance how to act in any circumstance, based on preestablished and tested rules. Contrast this approach with the inconsistency and unpredictability of trading responses based on emotions such as fear and greed.

Assume a system has an average win of $1,000, an average loss of $500, and 45% wins. After 100 trades, there will be $45,000 in profits (.45 × 100 × $1,000 = $45,000), and $27,500 in losses (.55 × 100 × $500 = $27,500). This leaves a profit of $17,500.

Now assume that a system has a 45% win rate, an average win of $1,000, and an unknown loss size. After 100 trades, it can be reasonably predicted that 45 trades will be wins, a profit of $45,000 will be earned, and 55 trades will be losses. However, the dollar value of these 55 losses is unknown. They may cost $11,000 (assuming an average loss of $200) yielding a net profit of $34,000. This would be great. Or, they may cost $82,500 (assume an average loss of $1,500) yielding a net loss of $37,500.

Or, it could be worse. Would it be better if losses could be of any size? Not really. Knowing nothing at all about risk means knowing nothing about the value of the system.

It is important to understand that without a definition of per trade and per strategy risk, it is impossible to trade any strategy intelligently, whether systematic or subjective.

This is where consistency helps the most. A good trading system consistently applies the same entry and exit rules. In turn, all things remaining constant (which, experience teaches, is not always the case), the size and frequency of profits and losses will stay reasonably consistent. Given such a state, it is possible to estimate the rates of profit and risk. Therefore, it becomes possible to trade.

Without a reasonable estimate of potential profit, it is impossible to know if it is worth trading. Without a reasonable estimate of potential risk, it is impossible to know if trading can be afforded. Without knowledge of potential profit and risk, it is impossible to trade any method intelligently.

The profit and risk profile of a trading system makes it possible to compare different trading systems with one another. Because of the varying profit levels of different trading systems and the diverse activity levels of different markets, the only meaningful comparison from one system to another is rate of profit versus cost of trading. The cost of trading is best defined as margin plus risk.

ENTRIES AND EXITS

A trade involves entering and exiting the market. Ideally, the trader should enter the market when there is some reason to think there is a better than even chance of making a profit and should exit the market when there is no more profit to be gained in the current trade. So much for theory. On to reality.

Definition: *An entry rule initiates a new long or short position.*

An entry can only occur when the system has no current position. Examples of buy entry rules (sell entries are the opposite) are:

1. The 5-day moving average crosses from below to above the 20-day moving average.
2. The relative strength index is below 20.
3. The daily close rises by 1%, and the weekly close rises by 1%.

4. Today's close is higher than yesterday's close plus 50% of the daily range.
5. Today's close is higher than the previous 4 closes.

Definition: *An exit rule closes out a current long or short position.*

An exit can only occur when the system has an open or active position. An example of an exit that uses opposite entries is: Close out a long position when the 5-day moving average crosses from above to below the 20-day moving average.

Definition: *A reversal rule closes out a position and initiates a new and opposite position.*

A reversal can only occur when there is a position. A reversal combines an exit and an entry. The current position is exited and enters a new and opposite position. An example of a reversal rule is: Close out a long position and go short when the 5-day moving average crosses from above to below the 20-day moving average.

Such definitions will help us to think more clearly about trading systems. It is quite common for many trading systems to exit a position based on a new and opposite entry signal. Such systems are always in the market, long or short.

Some systems have more than one type of entry rule. Others have exit rules that are different from the entry rules. The permutations are nearly endless.

RISK MANAGEMENT

The management of per trade risk is the next element in trading system structure. If the only rules of a trading system are entries and exits, the potential risk per trade is theoretically infinite. Practically speaking, open equity drawdowns in such types of trading systems are often large. Although per trade risk is a personal question related to the preference of the trader, it is also an essential part of the assessment and evaluation of the total system risk.

Definition: *A risk rule limits the amount of capital that can be lost on the day of entry, and on subsequent days.*

A risk rule may accomplish this by entering a stop-loss order when a position is initiated. Because of fast markets and poor fills, the actual dollars lost with such stops often will exceed the desired amount. On the whole, such stops perform their intended function and keep most losses near the expected level.

Overnight risk, the change from close to open, is the greatest cause for exceeding such stops. For no matter the stop amount, if a market opens well through the stop, the loss will be substantially greater than the intended amount. Fortunately, such large, adverse opens are not frequent.

Some trading systems actually perform better without risk stops. Most do not. Determining this is an empirical question that is evaluated through testing and research.

Risk on Entry

Risk on entry can be strictly limited to a specific dollar amount by using a risk stop measured in a fixed point or dollar value. Such risk, of course, is subject to increase due to fast markets and poor fills.

Definition: *A risk stop is the amount of capital put at risk at trade inception.*

Definition: *A dollar risk stop is an unconditional exit, at a loss, at a point equal to a dollar amount above or below the entry price.*

For example, assume a dollar risk stop of $1,000 (assume $1,000 is equal to 2.00 points), and a long position entered at 350. The sell risk stop on this long position is 348 (350.00 − 2.00 = 348.00). The sell stop is placed at the time a long position is taken based on the system entry rule. If price subsequently goes against the new position and exceeds the risk stop, the trading system exits the position with a $1,000 loss plus commission and slippage. A buy risk stop for a short position is the reverse of the sell risk stop on a long position.

Overnight Risk

The risk stop used to control entry risk is placed as a GTC (good 'til canceled) order. To do its job, the risk stop must be kept in place through the life of the position. However, this does not limit the per trade risk to $1,000. Why? Because of unlimited overnight risk.

Definition: *Overnight risk is the amount of capital set at risk by the dollar value of the change in price between today's close and tomorrow's open.*

If the market's opening price exceeds the 2.00 point risk stop by 10.00 points, it will be filled at the opening price with a loss 8.00 points greater than intended. Overnight risk is a more dangerous type of per trade risk. The only way to eliminate this risk is to close out the position every night. Understanding overnight risk is essential to overall risk management.

Trading Risk

Definition: *Trading risk is the minimum amount of capital put at risk over the long-term to be able to trade long enough to realize potential profit. Trading risk may apply to a single market or an entire portfolio.*

There are various ways to determine the amount of risk capital necessary to trade a specific system. The three most important are maximum losing run, maximum drawdown, and margin.

Definition: *The maximum losing run is the series of losing trades that has the largest dollar value.*

Definition: *The maximum drawdown is the largest equity drawdown, measured from the previous equity high, before a new equity high occurs.*

Definition: *Required capital is the sum of maximum drawdown, margin, and a safety factor needed to trade a system profitably.*

This will be discussed in detail in Chapter 10, "The Evaluation of Real-Time Trading."

Profit Targets

One way of protecting open equity profit is simply to take a trading profit once a certain profit threshold has been reached or exceeded. Such a threshold is called a *profit target*. Profit targets are set with *or better* (OB) orders.

Definition: *A dollar profit target is an unconditional exit, at a profit, at a point equal to a dollar amount above or below the entry price.*

The incorporation of a profit target into a trading system is an aggressive method of profit management. Its good point is that the profit once realized, is taken immediately. Therefore, it cannot be lost. Its bad point is that if the market continues to move well past the profit target, these potential additional gains are lost.

There are tradeoffs. Some trading systems that use profit targets are less profitable but produce a higher percentage of winning trades than those that do not. Sometimes, per trade and total risk are reduced and overall performance may be more stable. These differences again can be decided based on the trader's risk preference. Not all systems are improved by profit taking. It is necessary to calculate the change in both risk and reward before deciding its benefit.

For example, assume a dollar target of $1,000 (where $1,000 is equal to 2.00 points) and a long position at 350. The sell target on this long position is 352 (350.00 + 2.00 = 352.00). This sell or better order is set at the same time a long position is initiated based on the system entry rule. If the price subsequently goes in the direction favoring the new position and reaches the target, the trading system exits the position with a $1,000 profit minus commission and slippage. Another plus to target orders is that OB orders cannot have slippage. A buy target for a short position is the reverse of the sell target for a long position.

The Impact of Overnight Change on Target Orders

This target OB order is entered as GTC. To do its job, this order must be kept in place throughout the life of the position. However, this does not limit the per trade profit to $1,000. Why? Because of the unrestricted overnight price change. If the market opens 10 points higher than the 2-point target OB order, it will be filled at the opening price. Here, overnight gaps can work in favor of the trading system.

A fixed target price limit order is static. It does not change during the life of the position. It is insensitive to changes in volatility or in the strength of the trend. However, targets can be dynamic if they are defined as functions of volatility.

The Trailing Stop

Another way to manage profit during the life of a trade is to construct rules that continuously advance a stop in the direction of a profitable market move during the life of the position. This type of profit management is generally called a *trailing stop*. As the market moves in the direction of the position, the trailing stop is advanced to protect more profit or reduce initial losses.

There are two variations on the trailing stop. In the first variation, a trailing stop is only set after a position has reached a minimum profit threshold. The reason behind this is to give the trade enough room to accommodate adverse price moves that are within the system tolerances and thereby minimize whipsaws. The second variation is to begin the trailing stop from the first day of the trade. This approach seeks to maximize profit as well as minimize loss. Either approach may work best. Which is the most effective in a system is an empirical question answered by testing.

The positive side of the trailing stop is that it protects ever larger amounts of accumulating equity profit. The downside is that a system can be stopped out of a profitable position on a correction prior to an advance to a new profit high. Once again, as with the other risk and profit rules, the use is subject to risk preference and performance testing.

Definition: *A trailing dollar profit stop is a dynamic order that is set a dollar amount above or below a current low or high price representing a new equity high.*

For example, assume a dollar trailing stop of $1,000 (where $1,000 is equal to 2 points), a long position of 350, and an equity high of 356.00. The trailing sell stop on this long position is 354 (356.00 − 2.00 = 354.00). This trailing sell stop is placed with reference to a high price that has caused a new equity high. If the price subsequently goes against the long position and falls through the sell stop, the trading system exits the position with a $2,000 profit minus commission and slippage. A trailing buy stop for a short position is the reverse.

The Impact of Overnight Change on the Trailing Stop

A trailing stop is dynamic, changing as the market advances in favor of the trade. To do its job, a trailing stop must be entered each day throughout the life of the position. However, this does not limit the per trade profit to the amount that is currently protected. Why? Because of the overnight price change. If the market opens 10 points lower than the trailing stop, it will be filled at the opening price, converting a paper profit into a real loss. Here, once again, overnight risk can work against the trading system.

Entry Filters

To add a level of complexity, *filters* can be applied to entry rules. Filters are other market facts or indicators that are consulted to determine whether or not to take an entry presented by the primary entry rules.

Definition: *An entry filter rule accepts or rejects an entry offered by the primary entry rules on the basis of additional information.*

A *single, simple filter* can be applied to the basic entry rule. For example, if today's close is higher than yesterday's, then take buy entry signals. A *single, complex filter* can be used. For example, if today's close, high and low, are all higher than yesterday's, then take buy signals. Either *multiple simple filters* or *multiple complex filters* can be used. The main purpose of the entry filter is to increase the overall accuracy of the trading system's entries. This reduces per trade risk as well as trading frequency. Taken to the extreme, filters remove all risk by eliminating all trades.

There is no limit to the type, complexity, or variety of entry filters. A number of examples are listed for the purpose of illustration. Accept buy signals (sell signal filters are opposite) if any of the following are true:

1. The relative strength index is below 30.
2. The relative strength index has been below 30 and is now above 30.
3. Today's high is higher than yesterday.
4. The last buy signal was profitable.
5. The close today is higher than the close 20 days ago plus 10.00 points.
6. The close yesterday is in the top third of the daily range.

Furthermore, any combination of these filters can be used. Although often fruitful, the complexity and difficulty of testing such systems rise dramatically as the number of filters increases. Also, the likelihood of overfitting rises with the number of filters. To take this to an absurd extreme, a "very" overfit model would feature a "filter per day." Such an overfit model might feature fantastic profit in testing and random performance in real-time trading.

Money Management Rules

To this point, it has been assumed that one unit has been constantly traded. In other words, the trading unit has been held constant no matter the amount of equity, or the length of winning or losing runs.

Definition: *A trading unit is the number of contracts or shares that are committed to each trade, that is, the position size.*

This book will use one contract for one trading unit. When trading one market, the size of the trading unit is irrelevant except to the net amount of profit and required trading capital. What is relevant is that it does not change. Trade unit size becomes relevant when a portfolio is traded.

Definition: *A money management rule determines the number of trading units in each trade.*

Money management introduces the idea that the number of trading units can change in accordance with a rule built into the trading model. There are a wide variety of different money management rules to determine the number of units to trade. In fact, the various money management rules become an element in the trading system that may be explored empirically. The number of trading units can also become a variable in the trading system that can be optimized.

An example of a well-known money management rule is the Martingale strategy, famous in gambling systems.

Definition: *The Martingale rule doubles the number of trading units after each loss and starts at one unit after each win.*

There are a number of variations on this theme. One is Anti-Martingale.

Definition: *The Anti-Martingale rule doubles the number of trading units after each win, and starts at one unit after each loss.*

Another type of money management rule, trade size, is based on the size of the account and the size of the risk assumed per contract.

Definition: *Trade size is equal to a fixed percentage of account size divided by the risk per contract.*

For example, assume (1) a risk size of 5%, (2) a risk per contract of $1,000, and (3) an account size of $100,000. The trade unit would be five contracts (($100,000 × .05)/$1,000 = 5).

There are many money management rules. *Optimal f,* recently introduced by Ralph Vince, is another way of determining trade unit size based on the percentage of wins. They all share a way of setting the number of contracts or shares per trade unit based on some measure of trading system performance or price pattern.

Advanced Strategies

Strategies that combine or build on the previous risk management techniques are considered *advanced strategies.* One such strategy is scaling into or out of a position.

Definition: _Scaling into a position_ incrementally adds to an existing position.

Definition: _Scaling out of a position_ incrementally decreases an existing position.

An example of scaling into a position is adding one trading unit to a position each time open equity profit increases by $1,000. An example of scaling out of a position is removing one trading unit every time open equity increases by $1,000. An example of both scaling into and out of a position is adding one trading unit to a position each time open equity profit increases by $1,000 until maximum open equity profit is $5,000 on the oldest position and then removing one trading unit each time open equity increases by an additional $1,000.

SUMMARY

This chapter points out that the major benefits of a trading system are its quantifiability, verifiability, objectivity, and consistency. A trading system can range from extremely simple to quite complex. There is no performance benefit inherent in either extreme. Testing and verifying a simple trading system is dramatically easier and less time consuming than a very complex one.

The seven categories or rules of which a trading system is composed are:

1. Entries and exits.
2. Reversals.
3. Risk management.
4. Profit targeting.
5. Profit management.
6. Money management.
7. Position management.

The minimum requirement of a trading system is that it must have entry and exit rules. At its most complex, it can include rules from all seven categories.

4

THE RULES OF
SIMULATION

THE IMPORTANCE OF ACCURACY

The testing of a trading system using a computer is a simulation of
trading. As with all simulations, it can be accurate or inaccurate. An
accurate simulation trades historical data in the same fashion as it trades
real-time prices. The more accurate the simulation, the better the real-
time results are likely to be. An inaccurate simulation will lead to false
conclusions about trading system performance. Such a false conclusion
will most likely lead to real-time trading losses. This chapter will cover
the essentials for achieving the most complete simulation possible for
accurate testing of a trading system.

PRACTICAL CONSIDERATIONS

A number of practical considerations are necessary to ensure accuracy.
They are generally simple to handle with a computer; however, their
omission can lead to various distortions of performance. Therefore, it is
important to treat them with thoroughness.

Transaction Costs

Each trade has a fixed and variable transaction cost consisting of commission and slippage. While it is normal to consider commissions, the cost of slippage is not so obvious.

Definition: *Commission is the transaction expense charged by a brokerage firm to execute a trade.*

Definition: *Slippage is the transaction expense charged by the trading floor. It is an estimate of the difference between the price you wanted and the price you got.*

Slippage is a significant cost to trading. The degree of slippage depends on the type of order placed, the size of the order, and the liquidity of the market.

Definition: *A sell stop order is placed at a price below the current market and becomes a market order to sell when the market trades at or below it.*

Definition: *A buy stop order is placed at a price above the current market and becomes a market order to buy when the market trades at or above it.*

Definition: *A market order is an order to buy or sell at the current market price.*

Buy stop orders are placed in a rising market and sell stops are placed in a falling market. Often, stop orders are filled worse than their price because a stop becomes a market order with no restriction on price when touched. In a fast market, slippage on a stop order can be very large. Orders filled on the open will be done at the worst side of the opening range. This is just the way floor brokers fill orders without a limit. To be sure of an accurate simulation, it is important to be sure slippage is charged to any order filled at the high or low.

Definition: *A sell price limit order is placed at a price above the current market and must be filled at or above its price.*

Definition: *A buy price limit order is placed at a price below the current market and must be filled at or below its price.*

Buy price limit orders are placed in a falling market and sell limit orders are placed in a rising market. Price limit orders function in an opposite way from that of stop orders. Conversely, a price limit order must be filled at or better than its limit. Anything else is unacceptable. The trader should keep these facts of life in mind and use price limit orders whenever feasible. The drawback of a limit order is that it might not be filled if the market is fast or only trades at the price for a short time.

Definition: *A sell MIT order ("Market-If-Touched") is placed at a price above the current market and becomes a market order to sell when the market trades at the indicated price.*

Definition: *A buy MIT order is placed at a price below the current market and becomes a market order to buy when the market trades at the indicated price.*

Buy MIT orders are placed in a falling market and sell MIT orders are placed in a rising market. The MIT order functions in a way analogous to that of the price limit order and eliminates the drawback of a limit order that might not be filled under certain conditions. Because it becomes a market order, it has the drawback of the larger slippage associated with orders without price limits.

The significance of transaction costs is not great in a long-term trading system that aims for larger profit per trade. Assume a system trades for four years, makes 10 trades, and earns $20,000 in profit. Deduct transaction costs of $90 ($40 for commission and $50 for slippage) per trade from the $20,000 profit. This leaves $19,100 profit ($20,000 − ($90 × 10) = $19,100). This small change (4.5%) is of little significance.

The significance of transaction costs, however, is much more apparent in a very active, short-term trading system. Transaction costs can have a dramatic impact on the performance of such a system. For example, assume a system trades for one year, makes 200 trades, and earns a net profit of $10,000. At first, this doesn't sound too bad. Upon deeper examination, a flaw appears. There was no deduction for transaction costs of $90 per trade from the $10,000 profit. This charge "transforms" the $10,000 profit into an $8,000 loss ($10,000 − ($90 × 200) = −$8,000). This is a 180% change.

Limit Moves

Many futures contracts have trading limits. As most traders know, it is nearly impossible to buy into a limit-up market or sell into a limit-down market. To be safe, a trading simulation should not allow entries or exits on locked-limit days. A locked-limit day is one where the open, high, low, and close are the same and the volume is practically zero. Such a day does not facilitate trade. On such a day, the computer simulation must not assume that a trade was possible.

There can also be days when there is a small amount of trading before the market locks at the limit. These also are not tradable, and special care should be taken to identify these types of days. A day that locks limit at the high is identified by an equal high and close, and a high that is equal to the previous day's close plus the daily limit. A day that locks limit at the low is identified by an equal low and close, and a low that is equal to the previous day's close minus the daily limit.

Opening Gaps

All markets feature gap openings of varying size. The opening gap must be factored into the simulation. Each order must be first tested against the opening price. For example, if the system logic uses a buy stop to enter the market and the opening price is above the stop price, then the order would be filled on the open, probably at the upper end of opening range, regardless of where the stop order was placed. Assume a buy stop price of 345.00 and an opening range of 349.75 to 350.25. Then assume a fill at 350.25. Opening gaps will always work against stop orders. Conversely, open price gaps work in favor of or better orders. However, to ensure a conservative simulation, the fill price should again be taken as the worst side of the opening range.

Order Checks

It is important to check all orders properly in accordance with exchange rules. Stop orders become market orders when touched. Therefore, when checking during simulation, it is only necessary that the high and a buy stop price be equal and a low and sell stop price be equal. Limit orders are guaranteed to be filled if and only if there is a trade through the price. This is not guaranteed in a fast market. Therefore, when checking price orders during simulation, it is necessary for the high to be *greater than* a sell or better order and the low to be *less than* a buy or better order. Even in this case an execution is not guaranteed, but it is much less likely to be missed if the price is penetrated.

The number of contracts on an order also becomes a factor. The larger the size of a stop order, the worse the slippage. A stop order to buy 5 S&P 500 futures is easy to execute and a standard slippage factor will provide an accurate simulation. A stop order to buy 500 S&P 500 futures is a different story. A larger slippage should be applied to such an order.

In an analogous way, a price limit order to sell 5 S&P 500 futures presents much less of a problem than a price limit order to sell 500. The likelihood of a full execution of a larger order is much less than that of the smaller order and must be taken into consideration to achieve an accurate simulation.

Order of Execution

The order of execution of a series of contingent orders can dramatically affect trading performance. It is not a problem if a trading system only enters one order per day. It becomes a problem if a trading system enters more than one order per day and the data used in analysis is limited to the daily open, high, low, and close.

Assume a trading system enters one order per day before the open. No matter what the order, the computer must only test to see if it is hit by the open, and if not, if it is within the daily range. If either is true, the order is unambiguously filled. If both are false, the order is not filled.

However, if a trading system produces an entry order, and a contingent risk stop, the result can be ambiguous. The simulation checks the entry order against the open. If filled, it checks the risk stop against the daily range. This is unambiguous. However, it is not clear when the entry order is filled during the day. Why? Because whether or not the risk stop is filled depends on whether the high or the low came first.

For example, if there is a buy entry stop price of 352, a contingent sell stop at the fill price minus 2.00 points, a high of 354, a low of 350, and a close of 353, then the entry stop at 352 is filled. That much is clear. If the high came first, then the risk stop at 350 is also filled and the trade is stopped out of the market. If, however, the low came first, then the trading simulation will assume that the entry order was filled on the way up to the close from the low earlier in the day and the risk stop was not hit. This becomes even more important if more than two orders are submitted by the trading system. Therefore, to eliminate "overoptimism" in the simulation, the worst case must be assumed—that if the stop is within the daily range, it is filled.

The only way to test such intricate orders sequences with complete accuracy is with tick data, five-minute bars, or other short-term data. Unfortunately, it is not often done because of the unavailability of such data, the expense, and the slowness of the simulations. However, any trading system that depends on an intricate sequence of orders, or on orders that are very close together in price, must be tested using data that clearly identify price movement.

Significant Dates

Major economic reports and contract expiration can cause explosive moves in markets. As a result, it is the practice of many traders to exit positions on the eve of significant economic reports or expiration days. Some systems will benefit from the ability to avoid the risk of trading into these events.

In a similar way, many traders will suspend trading in a market after a cataclysmic event, when an outbreak of war or some other price shock generates hypervolatility. Some traders suspended trading in oil on the day after the first American air strikes in Iraq in January 1991. It is impossible to anticipate price reaction in a very sensitive, news-driven market. The risk alone, resulting from exceptional volatility, is often a good reason to stand aside. Such a feature can also be built into simulation software as an option.

It is helpful to eliminate the effects of very large unusual market events from a simulation. For example, any trading system that caught the October 1987 crash would have made an unusual, windfall profit. Such events are rare and normally unpredictable and should not be assumed as part of a clever trading strategy. Therefore, it is important to judge the performance of the trading system before and after this event, without the influence of this large, rare market opportunity. The ability to bracket such dates is also valuable in simulation software.

PRICE DATA

The type of price data selected for use in trading simulations is very important. Futures and options with a finite life caused by expiration are more difficult to test than continuous price stream instruments such as equities or cash markets.

Stock Prices

Because a stock is a continuously traded instrument (i.e., it does not expire), its price data can be used as is without complication. Stocks traded on the New York Stock Exchange and the American Stock Exchange are readily available from any number of data vendors.

One minor problem: Many vendors of stock data do not provide the opening price. A few do. To compound matters, most repeat the close price of the day in the open field; therefore, any trading system that uses the open price cannot be tested accurately with such data.

Cash Markets

Historical price data for many cash markets are also available from a number of data vendors. There are underlying cash instruments for all futures markets and cash markets for all major currencies. Cash markets are continuously traded, do not expire, and can be used for simulations. However, because cash markets usually behave differently from the instruments derived from them, it is not suggested that they be used as a substitute for futures prices. Use cash market data if you are going to trade the cash market and use futures data if you are going to trade futures or forward markets.

Futures Markets

A futures market consists of a series of contracts to be delivered at different forward dates. All futures contracts have a finite life. All futures contracts are delivered or settled on the last day of contract trading and then stop trading. They become the cash market. For example, the June 1991 Deutsche mark futures expired on June 21, 1991.

Because of this expiration, any futures contract goes through a continuous process of change in the way it is traded as it progresses through its "life cycle." The lead contract, also called the spot or prompt price, will be the most heavily traded of all contracts. Consider an illustration. In January 1991, the December 1991 live cattle contract will be the sixth deferred delivery and more thinly traded. There is less interest in a more distant contract because it is difficult to determine its correct price. It is always more difficult to assess how today's events will affect prices further out into the future.

Due to this "lessened interest," the December 1991 contract prices will have less volume, narrower daily ranges, and significantly more gaps in February 1991 than in the April 1991 contract. Figure 4–1 is an overlay of the February 1991 and December 1991 live cattle futures contract from 12/3/90 to 1/31/91. The difference is quite apparent. The first thing to note is that a distant contract has price features that differ from the nearby contract.

There is an additional and larger complication. When the February 1991 contract expired, the December 1991 contract moved up from the sixth position to the fifth deferred contract and it attracted a little more trading. As a consequence, its price characteristics took on a slightly different complexion. Another increase in trading volume occurred when the April 1991 contract expired and the December 1991 contract became

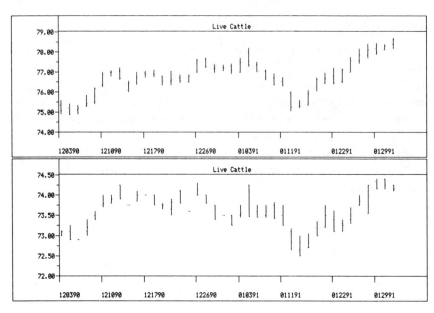

Figure 4–1 Top Screen: Live Cattle, February 1991; Bottom Screen: Live Cattle, December 1991

the fourth delivery. In fact, there is a continuous change in the prices of a futures contract from its beginning to its expiration. This change is natural to the market.

It is the limited life and changing profile that make the use of actual futures contracts unusual for the purposes of trading system simulations. The price gaps that occur at "rollover" (i.e., the transition from the expiring contract to the current active contract) must be treated as they would be in actual trading. The simulation must insert a rollover trade. Any open position must be liquidated in the expiring contract and may be reinstated in the current contract. This will involve one commission, slippage, and the profit or loss of the closed-out trade.

A number of other solutions have been offered that involve transforming the data in some way. But most of the solutions present additional problems as will be seen in the following sections.

Individual Contracts

The use of an individual price contract (i.e., the December 1991 live cattle futures) presents two major problems: It is finite, and it inaccurately represents the typical trading platform of most traders. Since most traders only use the most active contract, a simulation of trading that uses the calendar month January 1991 within the December 1991 futures contract will be inaccurate. Figure 4-2 shows the December 1991 contract from 1/2/91 through 12/19/91.

Trading simulations should be at least five years in length. Because the December 1991 live cattle futures contract only trades for about 18 months, it cannot be used for the entire test. For these two reasons, using full individual price contracts is not possible.

The Continuous Contract

One good solution to both of these problems is the *continuous contract*— a patchwork of successive individual futures contracts. In January 1991, a continuous contract will have price data from the February 1991 contract. In April 1991, it will have price data from the June 1991 contract. In other words, it follows the front price contract.

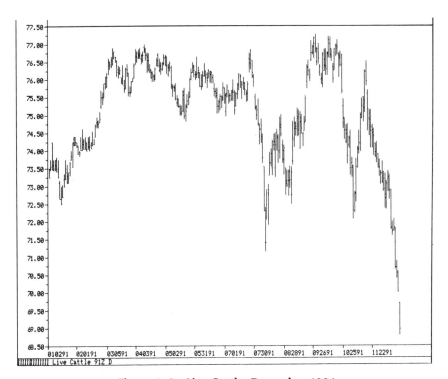

Figure 4-2   Live Cattle, December 1991

The continuous contract solves two of the three major problems. It can be as long as required. It represents the nearby contract price data and thereby accurately reflects the natural trading vehicle of most traders. It has one problem: The rollover price gap appears to be an opening gap, which can result in a windfall profit or loss when that situation never existed. The trading simulation must take this into consideration.

The Perpetual Contract

A popular solution is the *perpetual contract*. This contract is very different from the continuous contract; it consists of a mathematical transformation of price data, which is, consequently, *not* real price data. Prices in a perpetual contract are actually converted by an interpolation formula that attempts to create the three-month forward values of the commodity in a manner similar to the London Metals Exchange forward pricing. The transformed value is different for every day of the contract. The design of the formula is intended to provide a price history that is close to the targeted three-month contract.

The perpetual contract also solves two of the three major problems: It can be as long as required, and it is more similar to the front contract price data and eliminates the rollover price gaps. But it is not representative of nearby prices.

The perpetual contract introduces three unique problems. First, it does not contain real price history. Every price is transformed. Second, it introduces a new distortion of its own and it tends to dampen volatility. It behaves differently than the actual price data itself. Third, it is necessary to transform entry orders for real-time trading derived from it. This adds work in addition to the distortion. Due to the proprietary nature of the formula, there is no way to do this accurately. Furthermore, this added distortion may be of little consequence with a very slow system that trades big moves; however, such a distortion may prove to be a serious problem with a very active trading system that targets small moves.

Merged Contracts

The *merged* contract alternative preserves the best of all the preceding alternatives. A merged contract is actually a different way of loading price data. Instead of loading prices from one continuous price history as do other methods, the merged contract loads the pieces of price data that it needs from a series of individual price histories.

A merged contract may have two forms. The first leaves the rollover gaps in the prices that are loaded into the computer's memory. This is an *untransformed, merged contract*. There are two drawbacks to this. The simulation must properly handle all trades or any calculations that span this rollover gap. If it does not, performance will show windfall profits and losses. An untransformed, merged contract solves two out of three of the problems: It can be as long as necessary, and it is precisely the prices that are traded. Figure 4–3 shows a merged contract of live cattle futures from 1/2/91 through 12/19/91 with gaps.

The second type of merged contract removes all the gaps using a *neutral data transform*. Consider a merged contract of February 1991 and April 1991 live cattle futures. Assuming a rollover day on the last day prior to expiration month, price data will be loaded in a merged form from 1/3/91 to 5/31/91. The computer will first load price data from the April 1991 contract from 2/1/91 to 3/31/91. It will then load price data from the February 1991 contract from 1/3/91 to 1/31/91. It will calculate the gap between the February 1991 and the April 1991 data on 1/31/91. This price difference is the adjustment factor. It will then either add (if

Figure 4–3   Continuous Contract—Gaps In

the April 1991 is over the February 1991) or subtract (if the April 1991 is under the February 1991) this adjustment factor to every price field in the February 1991 data loaded from 1/3/91 to 1/31/91. In this way, the rollover gaps are eliminated. Figure 4–4 shows a merged contract of live cattle from 1/2/91 through 12/19/91 with gaps removed.

This neutral data transform preserves the relative differences between prices. It does introduce a distortion with any calculations that use percentages of price such as indexing. It cannot be used with charting applications that use absolute prices for support and resistance. The type of system being tested must be considered when deciding the type of data to use.

A transformed merged contract solves all three of the major problems for most systems: It can be as long as necessary, it faithfully represents the data to be traded, and it eliminates the rollover gap. It can introduce a slight distortion with trades that span the rollover gap. If the price data are taken very far back, prices can become unusually large or even negative, which will introduce a distortion in calculations using a

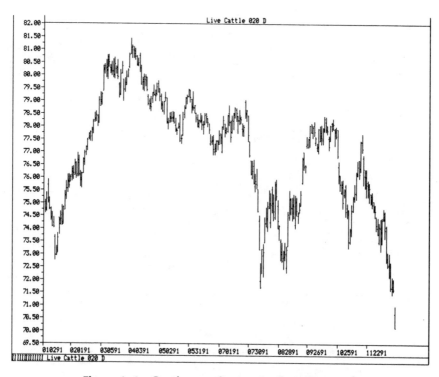

Figure 4–4   Continuous Contract—Gaps Removed

percentage of price. Merged contracts are, therefore, not appropriate for testing all trading theories.

Summary

Stock and cash market prices can be used in simulation testing without change. The only proviso is that many stock series are without an opening price. Some cash market prices are available only in close-only form. Simulations that require more cannot be done.

Futures prices are fraught with difficulties: Expiration limits their length; a synthetic series that spans the rollover will contain a price gap; and the natural life cycle of a futures contract renders it unusable. The four solutions all require some type of data manipulation. The two that offer no distortion at all but require more difficult computer work are the continuous contract and untransformed merged contracts. The two other solutions—the perpetual contract and the transformed merged contract—offer some distortion but greater computational ease. The transformed merged contract offers the least distortion and is therefore the preferred method.

THE SIZE OF THE TEST WINDOW

All trading systems are tested on at least one segment of historical data. For example, the performance of a moving average system will be tested on S&P 500 futures historical price data from 1/1/85 through 12/31/90.

Definition: *The test window is the size of that portion of historical price data on which a trading system is tested.*

Two main considerations must be satisfied when deciding the size of the test window. The first is statistical soundness; the second is relevance to the trading system and to the market. These two requirements do not dictate the size of a particular test window in days, weeks, or months. Instead, they specify a set of rules that can be followed to determine the correct window size for the particular trading system and market. One size does not fit all in the case of the test window.

Statistical Requirements

The test window must be large enough to generate statistically sound results and include a broad sample of data conditions. What does *statistically sound* mean? Essentially, two things. There must be enough trades to be considered statistically adequate. The test window must also be large enough with reference to the number and length of variables used by the trading system. If it is not, the test results will be statistically suspect.

Sample Size and Error

There is a formula for the calculation of statistical error. This statistical measure provides helpful information regarding the adequacy of trade sample size. The larger the trade sample, the smaller the standard error. The formula for standard error is

$$\text{Standard Error} = 1/\sqrt{N} + 1$$

where N is the size of the sample. Standard error tells us the degree of accuracy of our results. For example, if the average win is $200 with a standard error of 25%, the average win is really $200 +/−25%. In other words, our average win is most likely to be $150–$250. In the name of conservatism, it is assumed that the average win is likely to be $150.

Consider three examples of standard error based on different trade sample sizes of 10, 30, and 100:

$$\text{Standard Error} = 1/\sqrt{10 + 1} = 1/3.317 = 30.14\%$$

With a sample of 10 trades, the standard error is 30%. Plugging this value into the preceding formula, the range of accuracy of the average win is $200 +/−30%, or $140 to $260. A sample of 30 trades has a standard error of 18%. The accuracy range of the $200 average win is $200 +/−18% or $164 to $236. A sample of 100 trades has a standard error of 10%. The accuracy range of the $200 average win is $200 +/−10% or $190 to $210. From these examples, it is easy to see that the larger the trade sample size, the lower the standard error, and hence, the more reliable the results of testing.

How Many Trades?

How many trades are enough? In the case of trading system testing and the information presented in the previous section, more is always better. You cannot get statistical significance without enough trades.

This requirement can lead to a problem in the testing of long-term trading systems that trade infrequently. It is sometimes difficult with many types of trading systems to produce a large enough sample size. The only way to be sure of getting enough trades in a slower trading system test is to make the test window very large.

Other guidelines can help. When a test contains less than 10 trades, extreme prudence must be exercised in its evaluation. It must be fundamentally sound, that is, based on logical principles that would give confidence in continuing. Exceptional attention must be paid to all other considerations that promote statistical validity.

Stability

The *stability* of a trading system refers to the consistency of its trading. The more consistent a trading system, in each of its dimensions, the more stable. In general, the greater the stability of a trading system under a statistically valid test, the greater its reliability during trading. Chapter 8 presents in depth how to evaluate the performance of a trading model. However, a few highlights will prove useful here.

There should be a good mix of wins and losses. The trades should be evenly distributed throughout the test window. The smaller the standard deviation of the dollar value and duration of a statistically adequate group of wins and of losses, the better. The smaller the standard deviation of the dollar value and duration of a statistically adequate group of winning and of losing runs, the better. These measures of trading consistency are important measures of stability. The best test window size is the one that reliably produces this information.

Degrees of Freedom

Statisticians use the term *degrees of freedom* (df) as a measurement of confidence in the test results. The same concept can be used in test design by including the number of rules, conditions, and resulting trades in relationship to the amount of test data. Fewer specifications and more data give greater confidence.

Although the need for this evaluation is intuitively clear, there is no formula that expresses the relationship. The concept of degrees of freedom has not been applied to the area of test design. In order to arrive at a useful guideline, consider an extreme example. Using ten years of grain prices (e.g., 1980–1990), apply the following rules:

Buy on May 5, 1980, sell August 1, 1980; buy June 20, 1981, sell July 10, 1981; . . . ; buy May 21, 1990, sell July 30, 1990.

There are 20 rules (10 buys and 10 sells) that produce 10 trades (20 signals). In order to avoid overfitting the data, we could use the definition:

Degrees of freedom = Number of signals − Number of rules

In this case, there are zero degrees of freedom. There is also no forecasting ability in this seasonal method; it was all done with hindsight. It becomes clear that a system must have many more buy and sell signals than it has rules and conditions. For now, consider a safe estimate as

$$\text{Minimum df} = 10 \times (\text{Rules} + \text{Conditions})$$

Degrees of freedom may also be specified in terms of the number of data points used for testing; however, this measurement can be artificially bolstered. For example, a 30-day moving average should be tested on at least 300 days of data (again, a factor of 10). If this system calculates the trend using closing prices, the availability of the open, high, and low price does nothing to change the 300-day minimum.

Keep in mind that satisfying the minimum requirements is not as good as using fewer rules and more data to produce a larger number of trades. This all translates into a larger test sample, more accurate results, and a more robust system.

Frequency of Trading

It is an interesting fact of simulation that the test window size will exert a big influence on the pace of trading and on test results. A smaller test window can produce an adequate sample size for a short-term and more active trading system. In addition, most short-term systems will not perform well over a large test window because market patterns change frequently with respect to the parameters of the system. For example, optimum short-term trends may shift between 3 and 6 days. Conversely, only a larger test window can produce an adequate sample size for a long-term and less active trading system. The sample size of the batch of all smaller individual tests may prove statistically adequate.

Model Shelf Life

The size of the test window has an interesting effect on the "shelf life" of the trading model. Trading systems that use optimization require some type of periodic reoptimization to fine-tune the trading model to current market conditions. It has been shown that trading models optimized on a larger test window can go longer between reoptimizations, that is, have a longer shelf life. Conversely, shorter test windows require more frequent reoptimization. Hence, they are said to have a shorter shelf life.

The main reasons for this difference are structural. The time period between reoptimizations has generally been found to be some fraction of the original test period. This is highlighted by walk-forward analysis, which is presented in Chapter 7. A good rule for the size of the trading window is between $1/8$ and $1/4$ of the test window size. In other words, if a 24-month test window is used to optimize the trading system, then it can safely be traded forward for between 3 ($24/8 = 3$) and 6 ($24/4 = 6$) months. Other factors exert influence. This is similar to the concept that statistical forecasts offer less confidence the farther forward they are in time from where the forecast is made. (See p. 60.)

The reason a trading system must be reoptimized is that markets change continuously. Therefore, if market conditions remain the same, the trading system should not require any further reoptimization. If they change, reoptimization is needed. New data are introduced into the model calling for new specifications.

A short test window may only "see" one type of market, a small sample of market conditions. When optimized, this model has been adapted to this market type and set of conditions. When the market begins to change into something with which the model has no experience, there is no assurance it will continue to perform as it did during testing. Therefore, it will require reoptimization to adapt to the new, unfolding conditions. It is just this limited view of the smaller window that demands more frequent reoptimization.

Conversely, a longer test window will most likely incorporate a larger number of market types and a larger set of market conditions. By definition, it has experience with a larger domain of market data and is adapted to this larger domain. With a larger experience base, this trading system is more likely to be able to respond to new market types and conditions as they appear.

In general, a shorter window requires more frequent reoptimization, tends to be a little less stable, and is more responsive to current price action.

A longer window requires less frequent reoptimization, tends to be a little more stable, and is less responsive to current price action.

TYPES OF MARKET

Even the casual observer of markets is aware of the bull and the bear market. The bull market goes up, the bear market goes down. As in all things, there are degrees of bullishness, bearishness, and markets in between.

The Bull Market

Bull markets are advancing markets. Prices are going up. There are "typical" bull markets. If a regression line is drawn through such a market, it will have a slope of 25 to 50 degrees. Such a market will advance at a relatively gradual pace, is sustainable, and can last for months or even years.

There can be "roaring" bull markets as well. A line of regression drawn through such a market may have an angle between 50 and 70 degrees. Such a market looks as if it is exploding. Some call this type of growth "exponential," but it really means that the rate of price growth is also advancing as price advances. Roaring bull markets are rarer than mere bull markets. They are also less sustainable and therefore relatively short lived.

The Bear Market

Bear markets are declining markets, that is, prices are falling. There are also typical bear markets. A line of regression drawn through such a market will have a slope between 25 and 50 degrees with price declining at a relatively gradual pace. Such a market can last for months or even years.

There can be panic bear markets as well. A line of regression drawn through such a market may have an angle between 50 and 70 degrees, or steeper in extreme cases. Such a market looks as if it is in freefall.

Often these markets are called panics and are usually the result of mass hysteria in the financial markets. Hysterical bear markets are frequently violent and thankfully short lived.

The Cyclic Market

The cyclic market must be added to the classic bull and bear markets. This too is clear to see although less well known. A cyclic market can exist with or without an overall larger trend. As the name implies, a cyclic market oscillates within a price range. A market hits a cyclic low and rallies to the top of the trading range. It forms a cycle high and then breaks to the bottom of the trading range. Its primary characteristic when viewed over enough time is a more or less regular fluctuation between the high and low end of the price range. There can be a mild bullish or bearish "tilt" to the trading range or it can be without direction. If the trading range is large enough, such markets are eminently tradable.

The Congested Market

The congested or consolidating market, another major market type, is characterized by both an absence of trend and of volatility, or slow-declining volatility. A congested market consists of short-lived oscillations between the top and bottom of a very narrow trading range. They are typically untradable with systems that use daily data. They also have a more sinister impact on trading systems. A good trading system will most often show its largest losing streaks as the result of a congested market. In a very real way, congested markets are a black hole for profits.

Efficient Markets

The efficient market hypothesis (EMH) has enjoyed a great deal of support in the academic fields. This theory states that the market is efficient. It might be asked, "Efficient at what?" The theory goes on to state that all information that has an effect on the price level of a market is equally available to all players and is therefore very quickly assimilated.

The current market price is said to be the "correct price" based on all available information. It holds that because the market is efficient, no one trader can obtain any advantage over another. All market anomalies are quickly discovered and quickly eliminated.

It is true that free open-outcry markets are the most efficient markets in the world. Information about a market is quickly distributed, assimilated, and more or less accurately reflected by the price of the market. Prices are set as accurately as the opinions of the community of traders. However, the market is very big and exists within a wide multitude of time horizons. A market can have anywhere from thousands to millions of participants.

Experience has shown that if there exists more than one trader, there exists more than one opinion about the market. All professional traders have access to more or less the same information at more or less the same time. Different traders have different uses and needs from the market. The floor scalper only wants to accumulate a few ticks at a time. The floor day trader wants to grab the middle of the move on 5 or 10 contracts. The hedger wants to ensure against adverse price moves before either making or taking delivery on a product. The arbitrager wants to trade small deviations in the price difference between two related products. The speculator just wants to make money in any possible manner. A speculator can trade from minute to minute, day to day, week to week, or month to month.

As more is learned about market action, it is clear how little is truly known. The structure of price action is poorly understood. Over the years, technical analysts have accumulated a body of rules about many features of price action. These rules, however, are far from codified into a body of precise mathematical knowledge. Markets exist, and they can be measured. Accurate measurement is the first step on the path to prediction.

Time and time again, market opportunities have existed, have been discovered and exploited, and have ceased to exist as they became widely known. This is particularly true in the stock market where indicator after indicator has been discovered, popularized, and made useless. From that perspective, the market is efficient. However, the market is not omniscient. Nor do all the participants know everything about the market. As a matter of fact, the truth is quite the opposite. Therefore, the more deeply a trader analyzes market action, the greater will be the number of discovered opportunities. The smarter the participants and the greater the number-crunching power brought to bear on the market, the more original must be the research.

THE USE OF RELEVANT DATA

The use of relevant data is, at heart, a balance between two opposite requirements of trading system development, peak performance, and statistical validity.

Convincing arguments suggest that peak profit performance is achieved by a model with parameters adapted to current underlying market conditions. For example, let us assume that current market action is a strong bull market characterized by good volatility and an abundance of clear-cut price swings. Does it not seem logical that a trading model will perform with peak profit and minimum risk if its parameters are adapted to these conditions? But, how well would a model do if its parameters were adapted to a nontrending market with very low volatility? Most likely, the model would not do too well.

This, of course, would present no problem if markets did not change their characteristics from time to time. There are many ideas about this quality of change. Some traders believe that a market has infinite variety all mixed together and consequently does not change its fundamental nature. Others have expressed a completely opposite opinion. They suggest that one market does not exist; it is, rather, "an endless succession of ever-different minimarkets." Both are extreme views. There is truth in each of them.

Some evidence suggests that markets maintain certain structural features for long periods. For example, some would maintain that there are strong seasonal tendencies in the grain markets. Certainly, the grain markets are vigorously buffeted by weather conditions during the growing seasons. Yet within the soybean market, there are strong bull markets and extreme bear markets. There have been periods of very low volatility and trendlessness. There have been periods of high volatility and strong, classic bull trends.

In a similar way, many observers would say that the currency markets are among the strongest trending markets. As a consequence, they are much less subject to strong price swings within the larger trend swings. Yet, they too are subject to bull and bear trends. They also fluctuate between periods of low volatility and consolidation and high volatility and stronger trends.

And yet, there is strong evidence for the contention that a market is a succession of small minimarkets. The most obvious illustration is the never-ending tug-of-war between the bull and the bear. All markets have bull trends and bear trends. Less obvious are the nontrending periods of consolidation or indifference.

Complicating market patterns is the impact of changes in volatility. As markets reach higher price levels, volatility increases. When bull or bear trends terminate, their endings are often punctuated by highly volatile moments.

Bull or bear trends do not always end the same way. Sometimes a bull trend can be quickly and surgically ended with a one-day key-reversal and become a plunging bear trend. The reverse, of course, is sometimes true of bear markets. Other times, a bull or bear trend, especially if extended, can end in a long period of sideways, low-volatility consolidation.

Volatility can contract sharply from lack of interest in a market. After T-bills made a classic, high volume, high volatility 1,000-point rally in 1979, the market consolidated for months in a narrow trading range with very low volatility.

Contracting or expanding liquidity can have a dramatic effect on market structure. Illiquid markets feature small trading ranges and many gaps in price action. Such stop-running markets can murder daily trading models. Conversely, highly liquid markets feature far fewer gaps. When they do occur, they are more likely to be of some predictive value.

Markets do change from time to time. J. P. Morgan, the legendary financier and market operator, was once asked by a newcomer to trading who was looking for a hot tip, "What will the market do today, J.P.?" Morgan wisely and accurately replied, "It will fluctuate."

The system trader must judge carefully between seeking peak performance and statistical validity. It is clear from this discussion that a trader can benefit from optimization on "relevant data." However, what is the price that must be paid?

Earlier sections in this chapter have presented certain clear-cut statistical guidelines that must be followed to ensure the validity of a trading model. There must be enough trades, enough data, sufficient degrees of freedom, and a broad range of market types. The theory of relevant data implies that only data similar to current trading conditions should be used. This rule is likely to bring the trader into conflict with these statistical guidelines.

It is unwise ever to compromise the degrees of freedom. This is the easiest way to arrive at an overfit model. A shrewd and more experienced trader can possibly offset any danger from too few trades or data by trading a model on a very "short leash" in return for the higher rate of profit such models sometimes offer. In other words, a model that has compromised the rules of statistical validity might be quickly reined in if it is showing any danger signs.

Certainly, a model that is developed on a smaller data window will have a shorter shelf life. In other words, it will require more maintenance in the form of more frequent reoptimization and closer observation.

To a large extent, one of the strongest points of walk-forward testing is the ability to find and trade the best testing and trading windows for an optimizable trading system. With this method of testing, the effects on trading performance of different window sizes can be directly observed and measured. Because of the inherent dangers of using a small testing window, even to maximize trading performance through the theory of relevant data, I highly recommend doing it only within the context of the walk-forward test.

5

SEARCH AND JUDGMENT

This chapter covers the following areas:

1. Search methods.
2. Evaluation methods.
3. The assessment of the results of a test run.

These are the more esoteric and less understood aspects of the testing and optimization process. They appear dry. Yet their impact on testing and understanding the results is dramatic.

SEARCH METHODS

All testing and optimization use some type of search method that will dictate the number of tests to be performed and the order in which they will be done, and a range of time periods over which the strategy will be applied. A search method is a way of progressing through the different parameters specified by the optimization and selecting the best set of model parameters.

In other words, any optimization subjects a piece of historical data to a series of tests. The order in which these tests are performed may affect the determination of the best parameter set. This is one reason there are different. kinds of searches through what is known as the parameter space.

An individual *test* is one trading simulation on one piece of historical data with one set of model variables. A *trading simulation* calculates all the trades using the model variables and produces a number of performance statistics. An *optimization* or test run is a batch or set of tests. The successful result of such a test is a set of models that meet performance criteria. An unsuccessful test run may result in no models that satisfy minimum performance criteria.

The Grid Search

Consider a test of a two moving average, crossover trading system on S&P futures from 1/3/89 through 12/31/90. The first moving average (MA1) will be tested for values from 3 days in length to values of 15 days in length in steps of 2 days. In the parlance, the moving average will be scanned from 3 to 15 by 2. Seven different values will be tested for moving average 1:

| 3 | 5 | 7 | 9 | 11 | 13 | 15 |

The second moving average (MA2) will be tested from 10 to 100 in steps of 10. Ten different values will be tested for moving average 2:

| 10 | 15 | 20 | 25 | 30 | . . . | 90 | 95 | 100 |

The entire test run will consist of 70 possible combinations of these two scan ranges ($7 \times 10 = 70$). The test run is conducted as follows. To start, each possible value of MA1 is tested with the first possible value for MA2 as follows:

| MA1: | 3 | 5 | 7 | 9 | 11 | 13 | 15 |
| MA2: | 10 | 10 | 10 | 10 | 10 | 10 | 10 |

After this test cycle is completed, the test procedure advances the variable for MA2. Each possible value of MA1 is then tested with the second possible value for MA2:

| MA1: | 3 | 5 | 7 | 9 | 11 | 13 | 15 |
| MA2: | 20 | 20 | 20 | 20 | 20 | 20 | 20 |

This process is continued until each possible value of MA1 is tested with the last possible value for MA2. The final tests are:

| MA1: | 3 | 5 | 7 | 9 | 11 | 13 | 15 |
| MA2: | 100 | 100 | 100 | 100 | 100 | 100 | 100 |

Trading performance is calculated for each of these variable pairs of MA1 and MA2. The trading performance for each of these pairs is judged according to the evaluation types that govern this test run. The top models are those candidates meeting the evaluation criteria. If the criteria and the testing process are sound, these top models are candidates for the next round of testing. Figure 5-1 depicts the search of this variable grid space.

This search method is known as a *grid search*. The two variable ranges define a grid of variable combinations. Performance at each combination is evaluated. In other words, the entire grid is searched. This is the most common type of search method. There are many other types. The advantage of the grid search is its thoroughness. If every possible combination is evaluated, it is impossible to miss the best one, unless the evaluation method is unsound. This will be discussed later.

The drawback of the grid search is its speed. In small tests, as in the preceding example, run time is insignificant, especially with today's fast PCs. Assuming one second per test, a grid search of 133 tests would take only 133 seconds, or 2.2 minutes.

Consider, however, a 4-variable test. Assume a test of two different moving averages and two volatility bands (VB1 and VB2) around each moving average. This results in the following four scan ranges:

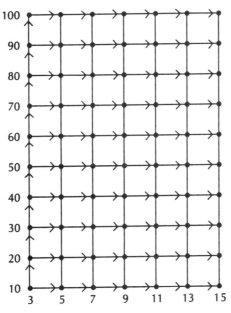

Figure 5-1   Grid Search—Two Variables

MA1	1 to 15	in steps of 2	= 8 steps
MA2	5 to 100	in steps of 5	= 20 steps
VB1	0 to 500	in steps of 25	= 21 steps
VB2	0 to 500	in steps of 25	= 21 steps

This defines a test run equal to 70,560 tests ($8 \times 20 \times 21 \times 21 =$ 70,560). At one second per test, this test run will take 19.6 hours ((70,560 tests/60 seconds)/60 minutes = 19.6 hours)! That is a long time.

To make matters worse, these variable scans are a bit "rough." It would not be entirely unreasonable to scan these four variables in smaller steps such as these:

MA1	1 to 15	in steps of 1	= 15 steps
MA2	5 to 101	in steps of 2	= 49 steps
VB1	0 to 500	in steps of 10	= 51 steps
VB2	0 to 500	in steps of 10	= 51 steps

This defines a test run equal to 1,911,735 steps ($15 \times 49 \times 51 \times 51 =$ 1,911,735). At one second per test, this run will take 531 hours (1,911,735 tests/60 seconds)/60 minutes = 531 hours). This is equivalent to 22.13 days (531/24 = 22.13). This, of course, is entirely impractical and highlights the main drawback of the grid search.

Therefore, to make larger scan ranges and 3- and 4-variable tests feasible, *search methods* must be used. A search method is a testing technique that selects variable combinations in a predefined way in order to locate the best set without testing every combination. There are many search methods. However, to gain speed, a certain degree of thoroughness is sacrificed. With each gain, there is some loss.

THE PRIORITIZED STEP SEARCH

The *prioritized step search* scans one variable at a time, with a selected value held constant for each of the other scans, in order of descending impact on performance. Consider the previous 4-variable test set:

MA1	1 to 15	in steps of 1	= 15 steps
MA2	5 to 101	in steps of 2	= 49 steps
VB1	0 to 500	in steps of 10	= 51 steps
VB2	0 to 500	in steps of 10	= 51 steps

As a grid search, recall the time required to makes this untenable. As a prioritized step search, however, it is quite manageable. It will consist of only 166 tests (15 + 49 + 51 + 51 = 166), which is quite a difference. How is it done? What is the drawback?

Variable one is considered the most important and is scanned first with a constant value for each of the other three variables. The constants for the other three variables can be chosen at random or a priori. A middle-of-the-road approach uses the midpoint of each scan range. The first scan will be:

MA1:	1	2	3	4	5	. . .	13	14	15
MA2:	53	53	53	53	53	. . .	53	53	53
VB1:	250	250	250	250	250	. . .	250	250	250
VB2:	250	250	250	250	250	. . .	250	250	250

In the first scan, all the possible values of MA1 are evaluated against constant values for MA2, VB1, and VB2. What is the impact of the assumption that MA1 is the most important variable? The first test will determine an optimal value for MA1, which will then be held constant in the subsequent scans of variables two, three, and four.

For example, assume that the first step in this test produced a top model with a value of 5 for MA1. The next step, the scan of the second variable will proceed using the following combinations:

MA1:	5	5	5	5	5	. . .	5	5	5
MA2:	5	7	9	11	13	. . .	97	99	101
VB1:	250	250	250	250	250	. . .	250	250	250
VB2:	250	250	250	250	250	. . .	250	250	250

This scan will in turn produce an optimal value for MA2. This optimal value, for example, 29, will subsequently be used in the third and fourth scans.

The two benefits of the prioritized step search are: speed and the assessment of the relative impact of each variable. The most significant model variable is the one that has the most dramatic impact on performance. Assume that a scan of MA1 produces the following results:

MA1	P&L	MA1	P&L
1	(−$ 3,000)	6	$12,000
2	$ 2,500	7	$ 9,000
3	$ 5,000	8	$ 7,000
4	$10,000	. . .	.
5	$15,000	15	(−$ 3,000)

In the same test, a scan of VB1 produces the following profits and losses:

VB1	P&L	VB1	P&L
0	$14,000	30	$14,000
10	$14,000	40	$13,500
20	$14,000	50	$14,500

VB1	P&L	VB1	P&L
60	$15,000	. . .	.
70	$13,000	500	$12,000

Different values of MA1 produced a pronounced change in profit and loss, whereas different values of VB1 produced little change. The conclusion from the data is that MA1 is a more significant variable in this model than VB1.

This can lead to two areas of action. Perhaps volatility bands offer little help to the trading model. Perhaps they can be eliminated. In model building, less is more. Certainly, given the small change that different values of variable VB1 produce, there is little reason to perform a more in-depth search. Given the small number of tests required to achieve this search, there is little cost.

On the other hand, the lack of thoroughness caused by the very limited scope of the prioritized step search can prove to be a large drawback in some cases, especially if the step search reveals that each variable contributes significantly to performance.

Direct Descent Search

The direct descent search is one of many very fast direct search methods. The main difference in the direct search methods versus the grid search is what might be called their "enlightened selectivity." A grid search simply looks at every candidate in a group of tests. A direct search seeks out the path of peak performance in the test group and follows it to its logical conclusion. Along the way, it rejects performance that is less than what has been found and favors better performance and moves in that "direction" within the set of tests or *model space,* as it is sometimes called. See Figure 5–2 for a graphic of this idea.

The benefit of the "enlightened selectivity" built in to direct search methods is that they are usually very fast. A direct search method may only need to calculate 5% to 10% of all the possible models, while a grid search method calculates the maximum number of combinations.

The direct descent search can also suffer from a lack of thoroughness. By not examining every model candidate, this method runs the risk of missing the best model. The direct descent search method also requires continuity in the model space. These methods can be fooled into selecting a local maxima as the global maxima. That is, it can select a top model for a particular area of the variable space and stop looking; consequently, it will miss the top model for the entire space.

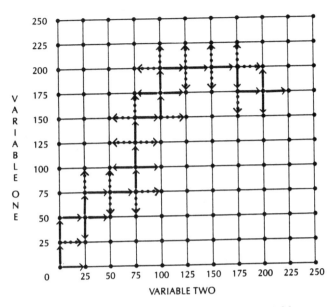

Figure 5-2 Direct Descent Search—Two Variables

A combination of a local grid search with a direct search method is a variation on the theme that combines some of the best points of both methods in a manner tending to offset each of their weaknesses. It is faster than a grid search and slower than a pure direct search. It is less thorough than a grid search and more thorough than a direct search. It is less prone to being fooled by local maxima than a direct search.

The multipoint direct search selects a group of different starting points. They can be chosen in a number of ways such as by picking them at random from the variable space, or by dividing the variable space into equidistant sections and picking the "center" of each section as an entry point. (See Figure 5-3.) The search then enters the variable space at its first point of entry and finds the best model in the area. If the search does not produce a candidate that meets the performance criteria after a certain number of predefined steps have been executed, the grid search of the local region is skipped and the search goes on to the next starting point. If this candidate does meet minimum performance criteria, a grid search is then done of this local region of the model space. The top model is found and stored. The search then goes on to the next starting point and repeats this process. If a candidate is found that meets performance criteria, a grid search of that region is done and the top model found here is compared with the top model found in previous searches. If it is better, it becomes the new top model. If it is not as good, it is rejected. The

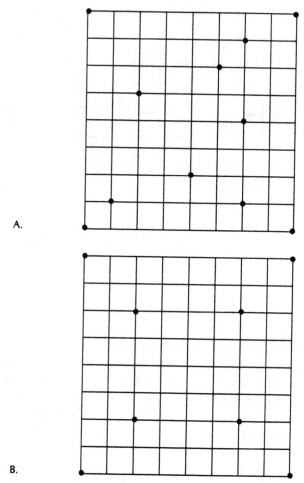

A.

B.

Figure 5-3 **A.** Random Starting Points; **B.** Equidistant Starting Points

multipoint direct search continues in this way until all entry points have been explored.

This combined search method is faster than the grid search and slower than a pure, direct search. It is more thorough than a pure direct search and less thorough than a grid search. It is less likely to take a local for the global top model than a pure direct search method. The analyst can choose as many starting points as desired; at its extreme, each point on the grid is a starting point and this method becomes the same as, but slower than, a grid search.

Genetic Search Methods

Genetic search methods are the most advanced and sophisticated of the new methods that have thus far emerged. Indications are that they are faster and more robust than any previous methods. The details of their operation are beyond the scope of this book. Their promise, however, makes it worthwhile to know of their existence.

Genetic search methods are a direct search method, but the inclusion of "mutations" (in other words, irregular random steps into areas of the variable space that are not on the direct search path) makes them less likely to select a local instead of a global top model. Because many trading model spaces tend to be spikey, the robustness of the genetic methods in such spaces recommends them for trading model research.

General Problems with Search Methods

There are some drawbacks to the direct search methods in general. Since a direct search method does not evaluate every candidate, there is a potential for a lack of thoroughness. A direct search would be far more thorough than a step search. It would be less thorough than a grid search. Experience with the multipoint direct plus grid search method indicates that it can reliably locate models that are in the top 10% to 20% of performers.

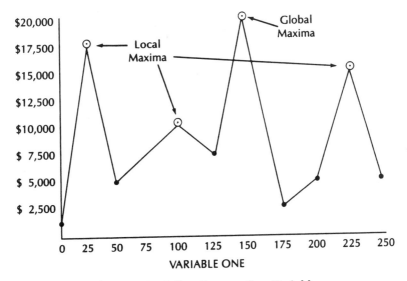

Figure 5–4   Spikey Space—One Variable

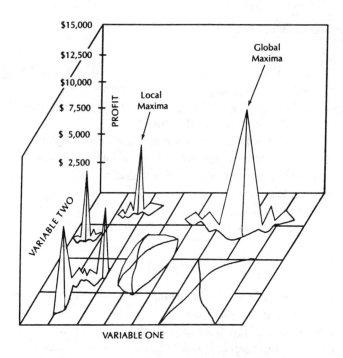

Figure 5-5   Global Maxima—Two Variables

A second and perhaps more serious problem with direct search methods is that they are not always guaranteed to find the true peak, called the *global maxima,* but can be fooled into choosing a *local maxima* instead. A global maxima is the best performing model in the entire test group, and a local maxima is the best performing model in a "local region" of the complete test group. (See Figure 5-4.) Mistaking the local for the global maxima can occur for reasons having to do with the actual design of the search method and the "shape of the variable space." Such a method will have a problem with a very "spikey" variable, a group of models with a large number of performance peaks surrounded by steep "valleys." (See Figure 5-5.) It is important to be aware of these problems when considering the use of a direct search method.

THE SIGNIFICANCE OF THE EVALUATION METHOD

Any search method must have some way to determine if a trading model is "good" in order to accept or reject each model. A good trading model might be the one with the highest profit, highest profit per trade, highest percentage of wins, or a combination of these three. Such a method of judging the quality of a trading model is called an *evaluation method*. It is also known in statistics as an *objective function*. What makes for a good trading model is far more than net profit. In fact, what makes for a good trading model can be rather complex.

Given the use of search methods, the evaluation type takes on a greater significance. Because search methods, by definition, are continually accepting or rejecting trading models in the process of seeking the best path, it is critical to use the correct evaluation method: It is that method which is most predictive of real-time trading success. The use of an incorrect or inappropriate evaluation type may ignore a sound model; even worse, it may select a poor model to trade in real time.

The best guide to the selection of the evaluation type is the proviso "Be careful what you ask for, because you may get it." For example, if *highest net profit* is the evaluation type, then the model that has the highest profit will be selected. After all, profit is what trading is about. Why then, is this bad? Because highest net profit alone is not an adequate measure of the quality of a trading model. For example, 60% of the highest net profit could be generated by a model with one large and (hopefully) unrepeatable trade, such as shorting the October 1987 stock market crash. Or, the bulk of the profit could have occurred in the first half of the test period and could be masking a devastating loss in the second and most current half. And net profit alone ignores the very important requirement that profits be evenly distributed.

Furthermore, the search for the largest net profit completely ignores the question of risk. The strategy with the highest net profit could also have a very large and unacceptable drawdown. Another weakness is that the top profit could be generated by too few trades. A model with such a small trade sample has limited statistical validity.

Net profit as a sole evaluation method ignores many important characteristics that must be considered in selecting the top model most predictive of future real-time profit. This discussion highlights some of the key characteristics of a true top model:

- Even distribution of trades.
- Even distribution of profit.
- Acceptable risk.
- Statistical validity.

The evaluation type should be designed to select the most robust and stable trading model, which may not necessarily be the most profitable. The objections to net profit as an evaluation type were chosen to highlight some of the factors that contribute to model robustness.

An unsound evaluation type can actually, and unwittingly, promote overfitting in the optimization process. An evaluation type that does not select models for their robustness calls into question the entire testing process. A robust trading model is most likely to produce real-time trading profit. A nonrobust model is most likely to produce losses.

A Selection of Evaluation Methods

The different evaluation types, both common and uncommon, are listed in this section, along with a brief description of each method's strong and weak points.

Net profit and loss is the net gain or loss of the model in dollars or some other currency unit. Although the trader is seeking the highest possible profit, net profit is an unreliable evaluation type when used alone. It can be unduly influenced by a single large win or loss. It completely ignores the number and distribution of trades. Net profit is an important element and can be used as a minimum criterion. For example, given slippage and other costs, a return of $100 per trade may be considered acceptable minimum performance.

Rate of return is an alternate way of expressing net profit and loss and a useful measure of model performance because it makes it easy to compare different time periods and different instruments. However, as an evaluation type, it is subject to the same criticism as net profit. It is helpful to set a minimum goal, but is unacceptable as a sole guide.

Maximum drawdown is a measure of risk and an important measure of model performance. It is assessed in two ways: the dollar amount of the largest string of losing trades, or the largest drawdown in the equity curve. In either case, it is a "defensive" criterion in that it is looking for the smallest dollar loss and not the largest dollar gain. Maximum drawdown as an evaluation method is subject to the same weaknesses as net profit and is therefore unacceptable as a sole guide. Maximum drawdown is helpful as a threshold. Models that exceed a certain drawdown can be rejected outright. However, minimum drawdown is not enough as a sole criterion, since a drawdown of zero occurs when a model has no losing trades and possibly no winning trades.

The *correlation between equity curve and perfect profit* is an evaluation type that implicitly includes the distribution of trades. More important is that this measure grounds model performance in the actual profit opportunities offered by the market.

Perfect profit is a theoretical measure of market potential. It is the total dollar profit resulting from buying every valley and selling every peak that occurs in price movement. Obviously, this is an impossible task, hence the name *perfect* profit. Mathematically, it is the sum of the absolute price differences.

The *equity curve* of the model is the cumulative value of all closed trades. Their relationship is defined by the standard statistical measure *correlation coefficient,* which ranges between −1 and +1. A value of −1 would be bad, because it indicates that as perfect profit is increasing, equity is decreasing. A value of +1 is good, because it indicates that as perfect profit is increasing, equity is also increasing. The formula for the correlation coefficient of perfect profit and the equity curve is

$$\text{Correlation Coefficient} = \frac{\Sigma(x(i) - M'x)(y(i) - M'y)}{[(n-1) \times SD'x \times SD'y]}$$

n	= Number of days in calculation
x	= Perfect Profit
y	= Equity Curve
$M'x$	= Mean of Perfect Profit
$M'y$	= Mean of Equity Curve
$SD'x$	= Standard Deviation of Perfect Profit
$SD'y$	= Standard Deviation of Equity Curve

The higher the correlation, that is, the closer to +1, between a trading model's equity curve and the market's perfect profit, the more effectively the model is capturing market opportunity. Why? Perfect profit is a cumulative measure and will therefore be growing throughout the trading period. A good trading model will also show a steadily rising equity curve. If a market becomes quiet, growth in perfect profit will tend to increase at a slower rate. The best model will also share a similar flattening or slow growth instead of a dip of the equity curve during such a period. Similarly, when market volatility picks up, it will be reflected in sharp growth in perfect profit. The best model will also experience strong growth in profit seen as an increase in the slope of the equity curve.

This measure, unlike net profit, will favor trading models that steadily profit at the same pace as perfect profit growth and that do not lose much when perfect profit slows. This is an excellent candidate as a sole guide. It is also a good candidate for a lower threshold.

The *pessimistic return on margin* (PROM) is an annualized yield on margin that is adjusted to "pessimistically assume" a system will win less and lose more in real-time trading than it did in testing.

PROM adjusts the gross profit by calculating a new, pessimistic, lower gross profit. The first step is to calculate the number of winning trades *reduced* by its square root or *adjusted* by its standard error. This adjusted number of winning trades is then multiplied by the average winning trade to arrive at a new, lower gross profit.

PROM next adjusts the gross loss by calculating a new, pessimistic, higher gross loss. The first step is to calculate the number of losing trades *increased* by its square root or *adjusted* by its standard error. This adjusted number of losing trades is then multiplied by the average losing trade to arrive at a new, larger gross loss. A new net profit or loss is then calculated with these adjusted gross profits and losses. This is, in turn, used to produce an annualized rate of return on margin. The formula is

$$PROM = [AW \times (\#WT - \sqrt{\#WT}) - AL \times (\#LT - \sqrt{\#LT})]/Margin$$

#WT	Number of Wins
AW	Average Win
#LT	Number of Losses
AL	Average Loss
Adjusted Number of Wins (A#WT)	$\#WT - \sqrt{\#WT}$
Adjusted Number of Losses (A#LT)	$\#LT + \sqrt{\#LT}$
Adjusted Gross Profit (AGP)	A#WT × Average Win
Adjusted Gross Loss (AGL)	A#LT × Average Loss
PROM	(AGP – AGL)/Margin

Assume a $25,000 annual gross profit, 25 wins, a $10,000 annual gross loss, 15 losses, and a margin of $10,000. According to standard calculations, this would be a 150% annual yield on margin ([$25,000 – $10,000)]/ $10,000 = 1.5 × 100 = 150%). PROM would yield a lower number.

Adjusted Number of Wins	$25 - \sqrt{25} = 20$
Adjusted Number of Losses	$15 + \sqrt{15} = 19$
Adjusted Gross Profit	($25,000/25) × 20 = $20,000
Adjusted Gross Loss	($10,000/15) × 19 = $12,667
PROM	($20,000 – $12,667)/$10,000
PROM	73.3%

This example clearly illustrates why this measure is termed *pessimistic*. It assumes that a trading system will never win as frequently in real time as it did in testing and that the system will lose more frequently in real time as well. It reflects these pessimistic assumptions in a modification of net profit using the standard error. As such, it is a more conservative measure. It is also valuable because it includes the number of wins and losses.

PROM is a robust measure because it factors in gross profit, average win, gross loss, average loss, number of wins, and number of losses. As its name implies, it pessimistically weights profit (by reducing it) and loss (by increasing it).

The pessimistic return on margin is a very good and robust measure of trading model performance. As a "pessimistically" adjusted return on margin, it is also a good way of comparing the performance of different trading models with one another.

There are two more stringent derivatives of PROM, *PROM Minus the Biggest Win* and *PROM Minus the Biggest Winning Run*. As their names imply, these measures adjust gross profit even further than PROM. PROM Minus Biggest Win removes the largest single profit from the gross profit and then calculates PROM. This is a more stringent measure than PROM. Its greatest benefit is to permit the evaluation of a trading system without the impact of the biggest winning trade, which may have been a price shock. Where there is no exceptionally large win, this measure is quite similar to PROM. However, where a large win was based on the stock market crash of 1987, PROM Minus the Biggest Win provides a measure of the model without this windfall profit.

PROM Minus the Biggest Winning Run removes the largest profit sequence from the gross profit and then calculates PROM. This is the most stringent measure of them all. It provides a measure of trading model performance adjusted for an exceptional winning run that might have been caused by unusually ideal trading conditions. In the search for the most stable and robust trading model, it is always best to prepare for the worst and hope for the best. A model that generates the best annualized return, both pessimistically adjusted and then without its best performance, is more likely to be robust in real time.

Multiple Evaluation Types

A combination of different evaluation types is preferable to a single measure. In this way, particular performance thresholds that contribute to robustness can be easily set. For example, rank the top models using PROM, and set the following criterion:

- Net return greater than $5,000.
- Maximum drawdown less than $5,000.
- A minimum of 10 trades per year.

Ranking the top models by a robust measure such as PROM will eliminate potential problems. Rejecting models that make less than $5,000 or have a losing run larger than $5,000 sets certain minimum performance criteria. Rejecting models that trade less than 10 times per year should ensure an adequate sample size. Ranking the models that meet these minimum criteria by PROM will yield the most robust results.

Evaluation Using Groups of Models

Performance spikes, or isolated profits, are the bane of optimization. A performance spike is a statistical anomaly. Consider an extreme case with a two moving average trading model. Optimization of one moving average produces the following performance results:

MA1	P&L	MA1	P&L
1	(−$14,000)	9	(−$ 8,000)
2	(−$16,000)	10	$ 4,000
3	(−$12,000)	11	$ 6,000
4	(−$ 8,000)	12	$ 6,500
5	(−$ 500)	13	$ 7,000
6	$12,500	14	$ 5,000
7	$ 3,000	15	$ 4,500
8	(−$13,000)		

The top model in this example is the one using a 6-day moving average and yielding a $12,500 profit. This does not look too bad in isolation. When considered in context, however, it looks different. One step on either side of the surrounding tests, to moving averages of 5 and 7 days, shows performance dropping off steeply to a loss of ($500) and a small profit of $3,000 respectively. Two steps further on either side and the deterioration of performance is extreme with losses of ($8,000) and ($13,000).

There is another performance peak at a moving average of 13 days generating a profit of $7,000. This is far less than the previous peak of $12,500. However, based on its surrounding test results, this one looks more appealing. One step on either side of the peak produces profits of $6,500 and $5,000 respectively. Two steps produce profits of $6,000 and

$4,500 respectively. This peak has profits on either side that are quite comparable to the peak performers. As a consequence, this secondary peak is most likely a more robust model than the first peak.

It is important to note here that a 1-day step in a moving average at small values is not equal to a 1-day step at large values. For example, a 5-day average is about 17% smaller than a 6-day average. A 7-day average is about 17% greater than a 6-day average. However, in the case of a 13-day average, the first 17% step down is an 11-day average and the first 17% step up is a 15-day average. It is valuable to understand this percentage stepping versus whole-number stepping, especially if large numeric ranges are to be scanned.

Some evaluation methods would pick the $12,500 model over the $7,000 (assuming profit is the evaluation type). There is a method, however, that reduces the effect of isolated performance peaks by averaging a model with its two nearest neighbors. The averaged model is then evaluated as an original entry. This smoothing tends to reduce the influence of isolated, and hence, nonrobust models.

Consider an average of the two performance peaks under discussion. The first peak of $12,500 had nearest neighbors of −$500 and $3,000. Averaged, they produce a new candidate of $5,000 calculated as follows:

$$(\$12,500 - \$500 + \$3,000)/3 = \$5,000$$

The second peak of $7,000 had nearest neighbors of $6,500 and $5,000. Averaged, they produce a new candidate of $6,167 calculated as follows:

$$(\$7,000 + \$6,500 + \$5,000)/3 = \$6,167$$

This smoothed candidate is superior to the first averaged candidate.

Evaluating the Test Run

A high-performing model surrounded by poor ones is unlikely to be a robust model capable of producing real-time profit. Such a model is more likely to be a statistical and seductive outlier. It was shown how a model surrounded by similar neighbors was superior to a profit spike. The overall performance of all the models in the test batch should be judged in a similar manner. Some guidelines are presented here.

The rules of statistical testing indicate that the best 1% of all test results are significant. This principle further indicates that 5% of all test results will be marginally significant. In other words, if enough darts are thrown at the board, a high-scoring grouping will occur. An optimization with only a few good tests will view these profits as statistically "significant," although the trader should be disappointed that the strategy was not profitable in general. Example 1 shows the results of a test run with less than 5% profitable results:

Example 1:   A Failed Test Run

Total number of tests	1000	100.0%	$2,458
Profitable tests	37	3.7	7,598
Losing tests	963	96.7	(2,457)

Based on this principle, if 1,000 tests of a trading system are generated, by definition the 10 best tests are "significant" and the next 40 are "marginally significant." A robust trading strategy should show many profitable results when the top 50 of the 1,000 tests are eliminated.

To have any hope of validity, at least 20% of the tests should be at a level of profit that is considered significant for the market and system. Example 2 shows such a result:

Example 2:   A Successful Test Run

Total number of tests	1000	100.0%	$5,447
Profitable tests	224	22.4	9,767
Losing tests	776	77.6	(1,983)

Of course, the greater the percentage of highly profitable results, the more robust the trading model is likely to be. Example 3 illustrates a robust test result:

Example 3:   A Robust Test Run

Total number of tests	1000	100.0%	$ 9,671
Profitable tests	671	67.1	12,671
Losing tests	329	32.9	(1,324)

The Distribution of Performance

Once a test run has passed the significance test described in the preceding section, it is helpful to review the distribution of overall test performance. This is accomplished by calculating the average, maximum, minimum, and standard deviation of all the tests. What is most desirable is a large average profit with minimum variation. The test batch with the smallest difference between maximum and minimum and consequently the smallest standard deviation is the best one. Example 5 shows the results of a simple trading model:

Example 4:   A Successful Test Run

Total number of tests	1000	100.0%	$4,523
Profitable tests	301	30.1	7,345
Losing tests	699	69.9	(2,993)

When comparing one optimization with another, the one having the highest average and smallest standard deviation is the best one. When making improvements or adding rules to a trading model and then retesting, it is important that the number of profitable tests improves, the average of the entire batch increases, and the standard deviation does not get larger.

Example 5 shows the results of adding a rule to the trading model reported in Example 4 that decreased performance in every category: percentage of profitable models, average results, average profitable model, and average losing model. Based on these results, this rule should be rejected.

Example 5:   An Unsuccessful Rule Addition

Total number of tests	1000	100.0%	$4,123
Profitable tests	221	22.1	6,256
Losing tests	699	69.9	(3,457)

Example 6 shows the results of adding a rule to the trading model that improved performance in every category: percentage of profitable models, average results, average profitable model, and average losing model. Based on these results, this rule should be incorporated into the trading model.

Example 6:   A Successful Rule Addition

Total number of tests	1000	100.0%	$5,798
Profitable tests	457	45.7	8,981
Losing tests	543	54.3	(1,876)

In Figure 5–6, A represents the test results of the first optimization. B, C, and D are different outcomes of a second test with one improvement added to the model. B is worse because it shows a higher average but a much larger standard deviation. C and D are different and both better than A because they both feature higher averages and slightly smaller standard deviations.

The Shape of the Test Space

Although the shape of the test space sounds like an abstruse idea, it is very helpful. The test space is a visualization of the results of a test

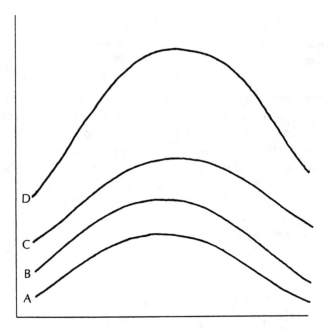

Figure 5-6 Optimization Test Results

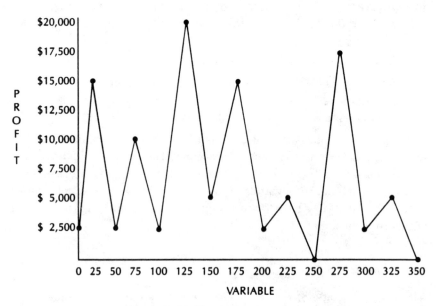

Figure 5-7 The Spikey Test Space

batch as a 3-dimensional graph. The worst case imaginable would resemble a mountain range of extremely narrow and tall profit spikes. Why is this bad? Such a model will lack robustness. Any small shift in a model parameter might change results from a large profit to an equally large loss. Such is the character of an erratic model space. (See Figure 5–7.)

The best case imaginable would be the top model resting on top of a big, round, gradually declining hilltop. This case is good because such a model will prove to be very robust. Any small or large shift in a model parameter will only erode performance by 5% or 10%. This is the strength of a robust model. Such a model derives it robustness from its relative insensitivity to parameter changes. (See Figure 5–8.)

An ideal 1-variable optimization should produce a profit performance line that gradually declines in both directions from its profit peak. An ideal 2-variable optimization should produce a circle with the best model in the middle and performance gradually falling off in ever larger concentric circles. An ideal 3-variable optimization should produce a circular hill with the best model at the top and performance gradually falling off in ever larger concentric circles declining from the top of the hill.

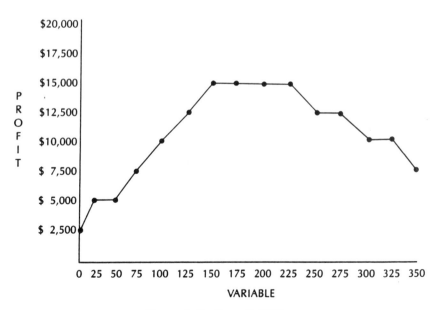

Figure 5–8   Smooth Hilltop

6

EXERCISES IN TESTING

The first stage in the development of a trading system is its design. This involves the development of a trading idea and then its implementation in some testable form. The second stage in this process is the preliminary testing of the trading model.

Testing comprises four main steps:

1. Verify that all the formulas and rules are being calculated as intended.
2. Assess whether the combinations of formulas and rules function as the theory would indicate.
3. Develop a preliminary idea of profitability.
4. Develop a preliminary idea of robustness.

Robustness is an important idea in trading model testing. The *Webster's II University Dictionary* provides the following definition: **Robust:** *Powerfully built: sturdy.*

The key word is "sturdy." In other words, a robust trading model is tough and long lasting. For our purposes, a robust trading model may be identified by three characteristics:

1. Profit over a wide range of variables.
2. Profit over a wide range of markets.
3. Profit over a wide range of market types and conditions.

In other words, a robust model will continue to perform profitably when markets change. Since markets change constantly, the more robust the model, the better.

Larry Hite, a top money manager, said in *Market Wizards* (by Jack Schwager, New York Institute of Finance, New York, NY): *We are not looking for the optimum method; we are looking for the hardiest method.*

Read *robust* for *hardiest*. A trading model that only makes money in T-bonds in a roaring bull market with high volatility and a very narrow parameter set is a trading model that is not likely to serve the interests of a trader who intends to trade for the long term.

PRELIMINARY TESTING

To check the design of a trading system, two things must be verified: the calculations and the trades. Even after years of experience, the best programmers and system designers must still make this crucial test. (See Figure 6–1.)

Doing this requires a performance test on one market and one chunk of data. The data sample must be large enough so that every formula and rule of the trading model are used to produce at least one buy and sell signal. It is necessary to use values for the model that are "reasonable" based on theory or experience. The design check must produce two forms of output: numeric details of all values that are used to calculate the indicators, rules, and trades, and a list of all trades.

Calculations

A detailed review of all the variables, rules, entry, and exit orders should prove that the trades are being generated by the correct formulas and rules. The only way to accomplish this is to compare hand calculations with those made by the computer. It is sufficient to spot-check these calculations by including at least one instance of each possible calculation. In Figure 6–2, the values for a 5-day moving average are presented with the daily closes to be spot checked.

Consider a moving average trading model consisting of two moving averages and a 2-day time filter. A 2-day time filter requires that the signal remain true for the length of time set by the filter; that is, a crossover remains true for 2 days. The model buys at the open when MA1, the 3-day moving average of closes, has been higher than MA2,

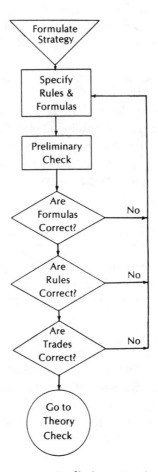

Figure 6–1   Preliminary Testing

the 12-day moving average of midpoints for 2 days. The model sells at the open when MA1 has been lower than MA2 for 2 days.

The first calculations that must be hand checked are those of the 3-day close moving average and the 12-day midpoint moving average. The next items that must be checked are the buy signal conditions: The model must have bought at the opening price, and only after the value of MA1 has been greater than the value of MA2 for 2 days. The final element that must be checked are the sell signal conditions: the model sold at the open and only after MA1 has been under MA2 for 2 days.

If any calculations are incorrect or the rules are functioning improperly, make the necessary adjustments. Repeat this test, check, and adjustment process until all calculations and rules are working as intended. Once all items are correct, go on to the next stage of testing.

Close = 62.11	5-Day MA = 62.5880
Close = 61.45	5-Day MA = 62.3419
Close = 61.50	5-Day MA = 62.0900
Close = 61.63	5-Day MA = 61.8759
Close = 62.37	5-Day MA = 61.8120
Close = 61.72	5-Day MA = 61.7340
Close = 61.85	5-Day MA = 61.8139
Close = 61.12	5-Day MA = 61.7379
Close = 62.89	5-Day MA = 61.9899
Close = 62.89	5-Day MA = 62.0940

Figure 6-2   5-Day Moving Average

Trade List

A trade list, as it sounds, is a tabular report with the date, buy and sell, price and the resulting profit or loss of each closed trade (see Figure 6-3). The next step is an evaluation of the trade list to prove that the model is buying when and where it should be buying and selling when and where it is designed to sell. In other words, the model is doing what it was intended it should do. This larger, macroscopic performance check will reveal any other anomalies that might have eluded the microscopic hand check of a limited number of buy and sell signals.

```
================================================================================
                    Advanced Trader V1.09 Analysis Report
--------------------------------------------------------------------------------
Contract Traded  : Swiss Franc          D 03/92          06/02/89 - 12/31/91
Script Name      : C:\PARDO\RPAT\MA00.LOG
Trades Analyzed  : All

Trade Order ! Type ! Entry ! Price  !! Trade Order ! Type ! Exit  ! Price  ! Net P&L
--------------------------------------------------------------------------------
O# 2    : 1 Sell ! 08/10/89 !  60.10 !! O# 1    : Buy ! 09/27/89 !  60.05 ! [$    37.50]
O# 1    : 1 Buy  ! 09/27/89 !  60.05 !! O# 2    : Sell ! 11/16/89 !  59.55 ! [$   725.00]
O# 2    : 1 Sell ! 11/16/89 !  59.55 !! O# 1    : Buy ! 11/24/89 !  60.45 ! [$  1225.00]
O# 1    : 1 Buy  ! 11/24/89 !  60.45 !! O# 2    : Sell ! 03/05/90 !  64.63 ! $  5125.00
O# 2    : 1 Sell ! 03/05/90 !  64.63 !! O# 1    : Buy ! 04/05/90 !  64.54 ! $    12.50
O# 1    : 1 Buy  ! 04/05/90 !  64.54 !! O# 2    : Sell ! 06/11/90 !  67.44 ! $  3525.00
O# 2    : 1 Sell ! 06/11/90 !  67.44 !! O# 1    : Buy ! 06/19/90 !  68.47 ! [$  1387.50]
O# 1    : 1 Buy  ! 06/19/90 !  68.47 !! O# 2    : Sell ! 09/26/90 !  74.55 ! $  7500.00
O# 2    : 1 Sell ! 09/26/90 !  74.55 !! O# 1    : Buy ! 09/28/90 !  75.23 ! [$   950.00]
O# 1    : 1 Buy  ! 09/28/90 !  75.23 !! O# 2    : Sell ! 12/03/90 !  75.55 ! $   300.00
O# 2    : 1 Sell ! 12/03/90 !  75.55 !! O# 1    : Buy ! 12/13/90 !  77.41 ! [$  2425.00]
O# 1    : 1 Buy  ! 12/13/90 !  77.41 !! O# 2    : Sell ! 12/17/90 !  76.41 ! [$  1350.00]
O# 2    : 1 Sell ! 12/17/90 !  76.41 !! O# 1    : Buy ! 01/22/91 !  77.95 ! [$  2025.00]
O# 1    : 1 Buy  ! 01/22/91 !  77.95 !! O# 2    : Sell ! 02/22/91 !  76.58 ! [$  1812.50]
O# 2    : 1 Sell ! 02/22/91 !  76.58 !! O# 1    : Buy ! 05/16/91 !  68.17 ! $ 10412.50
O# 1    : 1 Buy  ! 05/16/91 !  68.17 !! O# 2    : Sell ! 05/23/91 !  66.63 ! [$  2025.00]
O# 2    : 1 Sell ! 05/23/91 !  66.63 !! O# 1    : Buy ! 07/24/91 !  64.08 ! $  3087.50
O# 1    : 1 Buy  ! 07/24/91 !  64.08 !! O# 2    : Sell ! 10/17/91 !  65.65 ! $  1862.50
O# 2    : 1 Sell ! 10/17/91 !  65.65 !! O# 1    : Buy ! 11/04/91 !  68.08 ! [$  3137.50]
                                                   Net Profit/Loss     ! $ 14725.00
O# 1    : 1 Buy  ! 11/04/91 !  68.08 !!      open position             ! $  6150.00
--------------------------------------------------------------------------------
```

Figure 6-3   Trade List

For example, if the model is a simple close and moving average crossover, be sure that it buys every time the close today is higher than the moving average and sells every time the close today is lower than the moving average. If it is not, make the necessary corrections and rerun this test.

Summary

To summarize, preliminary testing consists of two things:

- A "spot" hand check of the various computer calculations of rules and formulas.
- A verification of each trade.

After these two essential verifications have been done, proceed to the next step.

THE THEORY CHECK

The performance of the trading model must now be evaluated in light of theoretical expectations (see Figure 6–4). It must be determined if preliminary testing generally supports or contradicts the basic theory. Assume that the theoretical objective is to trade swings of intermediate degree with a delay to reduce false signals. Such a model should have a few obvious characteristics: a moderate number of trades, reduced whipsaws, and moderately large profits. If trading performance generally conforms to this profile, then the trading model is performing in accordance with theoretical expectations. Go on to the next step.

If, however, trading performance deviates dramatically from this profile (e.g., trades are too long, profits are small, or too many losses occur), the cause must be determined. Was the theory wrong? If this is so, then does the unusual profitability of this "mutant" trading system warrant further evaluation as an entirely different trading system? When doing research, keep in mind that many significant scientific discoveries were the results of mistakes. If evaluation is appropriate, explore this as a new system. If not, reassess the structure of the model. Redesign the trading model keeping theoretical considerations in mind. Repeat the testing process. Do not stop looking for problems because one has been found; follow the entire sequence of events as far as possible.

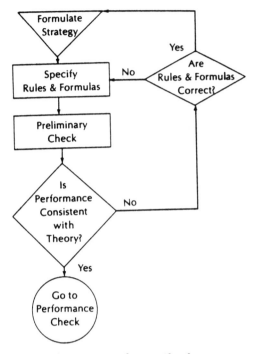

Figure 6–4   Theory Check

Note whether the price data were extremely "hostile" to the under-lying trading theory. This can cause a deviation between theoretical expectation and empirical results. For example, was a trend-following system traded on price data that included an extended period of conges-tion? If so, it might obviate the need for outright rejection of the trading model. It can be reason for rejection if the theory indicated different performance in "stormy weather." What is really happening is a test of the model under adverse conditions. If performance adheres to theoreti-cal expectations in this type of condition, testing can be continued. If not, go back to the design phase and evaluate the trading model in light of this new information. Retest if a design change can be made to solve this problem. Otherwise, the model must be rejected.

THE PERFORMANCE CHECK

The first test of the trading system is to calculate profit and loss on a current piece of price history of significant length, that is, one year for

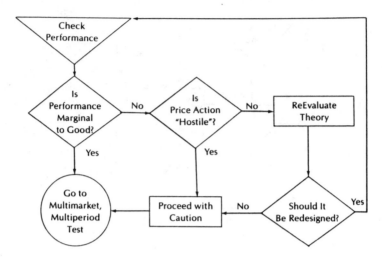

Figure 6–5   Performance Check

a short-term system, two years for an intermediate, and five years for the long term (see Figure 6–5). This first test provides a preliminary look at profit and risk. A general rule is to expect an annual profit equal to the margin required to trade the market. Risk should not exceed annual profit. Due to its very limited scope, it is incorrect to ascribe tremendous significance to profit performance at this stage (see Figure 6–6).

Performance is acceptable if it yields a marginal gain or loss. Marginal performance includes returns that are at or modestly below preliminary expectations. A test that yields a very high profit and accuracy with a very low risk is, of course, very promising, especially if its profile conforms closely with theoretical expectation. In both these cases, the test would be considered a success. Go to the next round of testing.

Performance yielding an unusually high loss is a warning sign. As discussed earlier, this can occur due to very "hostile" market conditions. If this is determined to be the case, go on to the next round of testing (see Figure 6–7).

If this large loss occurs under market conditions that are not terribly unusual, or even worse, ideal for the trading model, this strategy should be abandoned even at this early stage. The theory is clearly wrong. For example, a moving average model that loses money in a strongly trending market is a poor model. The only reason not to abandon the model completely at this stage is the narrow range of this test. If there is reason to believe this is an anomaly, go on to the next round of testing. If not, abandon ship. Back to the drawing board.

```
================================================================
                  Advanced Trader V1.09 Analysis Report
----------------------------------------------------------------
Contract Traded : Swiss Franc        D 03/92        06/02/89 - 12/31/91
Script Name     : C:\PARDO\RPAT\MAOO.LOG
Trades Analyzed : All
Dollar Factor   :   1250.00 Beg. Balance :   25000.00 Interest   :      0.00
Commission      :     50.00 Slippage     :      50.00 Margin     :  10000.00
Maximum Lots    :       1 Equity Limit   :       0.00 Max. Positions:     0

Inside Days Filter          :   No !  Outside Days Filter      :   No !
Extreme Outside Filter      :   No !  Extreme Outside Day Perc :  1000 !
Period of Daily Range Ave   :   10 !  Peak & Valley Level      :    1 !
Net Profit/Loss $  14725.00
Total Profit     $ 31825.00   Total Loss $ -17100.00   Avg. Trade $   775.00
----------------------------------------------------------------
              : # Trades !   Maximum    !   Minimum    !   Average
----------------------------------------------------------------
Total ........ :    19   :  Win  8/ 42% : Loss 11/ 57% :
Win .......... :     8   :    10412.50  :      12.50   :   3978.13
Win runs ..... :     5   :    10412.50/ 1 :   300.00/ 1 :   6365.00/ 1
Loss ......... :    11   :    -3137.50  :     -37.50   :  -1554.55
Loss runs .... :     6   :    -7612.50/ 4 :  -950.00/ 1 :  -2850.00/ 1
Win/Loss Ratio. :        :       3.32   :      0.33    :      2.56
----------------------------------------------------------------
Open Equity ......... $   6150.00   Open Equity Drawdown . $  -3225.00
Max. Balance Drawback $  -7612.50   Max. Equity Profit ... $  17862.50
Reward / Risk ........    1.93 TO 1  Annual rate of return.     46.89
Profit Index .........    1.86
Pessimistic Margin....  -16.83      Adjusted Pess. Margin.    -89.37
Pess. Month Avg.......  -24.42      Pess. Month Variance .     26.96
Monthly Net PL Large . 10412.50/9102 Monthly Net PL Small . -5800.00/9012
Monthly Net PL Ave ...  1132.69     Modified Pess. Margin.    -89.37
================================================================
```

Figure 6-6 Analysis Report—Preliminary Profits

```
================================================================
                  Advanced Trader V1.09 Analysis Report
----------------------------------------------------------------
Contract Traded : Swiss Franc        D 03/92        06/02/89 - 12/31/91
Script Name     : C:\PARDO\RPAT\MAOO.LOG
Trades Analyzed : All
Dollar Factor   :   1250.00 Beg. Balance :   25000.00 Interest   :      0.00
Commission      :     50.00 Slippage     :      50.00 Margin     :  10000.00
Maximum Lots    :       1 Equity Limit   :       0.00 Max. Positions:     0

Inside Days Filter          :   No !  Outside Days Filter      :   No !
Extreme Outside Filter      :   No !  Extreme Outside Day Perc :  1000 !
Period of Daily Range Ave   :   10 !  Peak & Valley Level      :    1 !
Net Profit/Loss $ -38287.50
Total Profit     $  75037.50   Total Loss $-113325.00   Avg. Trade $  -158.21
----------------------------------------------------------------
              : # Trades !   Maximum    !   Minimum    !   Average
----------------------------------------------------------------
Total ........ :   242   :  Win 96/ 39% : Loss 146/ 60% :
Win .......... :    96   :    5275.00   :     12.50    :    781.64
Win runs ..... :    59   :    5275.00/ 1 :   12.50/ 1  :   1271.82/ 1
Loss ......... :   146   :   -3325.00   :      0.00    :   -776.20
Loss runs .... :    58   :   -9287.50/12 :  -25.00/ 1  :  -1953.88/ 2
Win/Loss Ratio. :        :      1.59    :     12.50    :      1.01
----------------------------------------------------------------
Open Equity ......... $  -4150.00   Open Equity Drawdown . $  -4450.00
Max. Balance Drawback $ -40837.50   Max. Equity Profit ... $    762.50
Reward / Risk ........    0.00 TO 1  Annual rate of return.    -95.32
Profit Index .........    0.66
Pessimistic Margin....  -553.25     Adjusted Pess. Margin.   -600.99
Pess. Month Avg.......  -42.10      Pess. Month Variance .     31.07
Monthly Net PL Large . 6537.50/9102 Monthly Net PL Small . -7262.50/9008
Monthly Net PL Ave ... -1235.08     Modified Pess. Margin.   -600.99
================================================================
```

Figure 6-7 Failed Model

THE MULTIMARKET AND MULTIPERIOD TEST

The multimarket, multiperiod test is an expansion of the performance check in the dimensions of markets and history (see Figure 6–8). A test is performed with one set of selected model parameters on a variety of different markets and different historical periods for each market. The purpose of the multimarket and multiperiod test is to obtain a preliminary idea of model robustness and a broader view of profitability than that provided by the previous tests.

A test of the trading model on a variety of different markets assumes that the trading model was intended to be an all-market model. Of course, there are valid trading models that are intended to work on

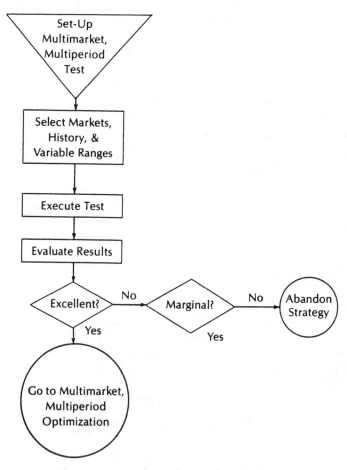

Figure 6–8   Multimarket, Multiperiod Test

specific markets. If this is the case, the multiperiod test must be done, but the multimarket test would be ignored.

If the trading model is an all-market model, then it is best to select 10 markets that are different from each other. Selecting the S&P 500, the NYFE Index, and the Major Market Index offers little diversity. A selection of Swiss francs, Deutsche marks, and Japanese yen would be rejected for the same reason.

Selecting the Basket

The criteria to decide the degree of difference include both statistical correlation and fundamental diversity. A calculation of the correlation coefficient between the closing prices of two markets will measure the degree of similarity between them. If the correlation coefficient is +1, they are perfectly correlated and should be rejected. If the coefficient is negative, they are inversely correlated and should be included. A coefficient between 0 and +.5 indicates that they have little correlation and they can be included.

A knowledge of the fundamentals of the selected test basket is easier and can prove helpful. Different fundamental conditions underlay coffee, cattle, and the stock market, making them good candidates for the same portfolio. It is also helpful to note the interrelationships of these markets under certain conditions such as a strong U.S. dollar or inflation.

A good test basket might consist of coffee, cotton, crude oil, gold, pork bellies, soybeans, S&P 500, sugar, Swiss francs, and T-bonds. A smaller test basket can include coffee, cotton, crude oil, S&P 500, and T-bonds. If the intention is to trade the model on a diversified portfolio, then the preliminary basket must be as diverse as possible.

Selecting the Period

The next step is to determine the minimum number of years of price history per market on which to test the trading model. The more, the better. Ten years of price history per market is a very good test. Five years per market is the minimum to obtain a reasonable trade sample size and some mix of market types. It is necessary to include at least one bull, bear, and sideways market in the data selected.

The first question that must be answered is whether enough data is available for testing purposes. In the case of S&P 500 futures, no. It began trading in 1983. Those who wish to be as thorough as possible might substitute the S&P spot prices for the early years prior to futures trading. In the case of the other nine in the basket, data exist. If the test were to be for 20 years, all financial futures that only began trading in the mid-1970s would be eliminated. Therefore, the amount of data that can be tested is a question of availability. The structure and type of testing to be done must be designed to work within these constraints. If a long-term test on the S&P 500 requires data prior to 1983, then cash data must be used prior to 1983. The following chart shows futures price data available from Technical Tools:

Aluminum	12/08/83	Oats	08/07/74
Australian Dollar	01/13/87	Orange Juice	08/22/72
British Pound	02/13/75	Palladium	11/01/82
Canadian Dollar	01/17/77	Platinum	08/22/72
Cocoa (Metric)	12/19/79	Pork Bellies	03/18/69
Coffee	08/17/73	Rough Rice	08/20/86
Copper	08/22/72	Russell 2000	09/10/87
Copper, High Grade	08/01/88	S&P 500 Index	04/21/82
Consumer Price	06/21/85	Silver (COMEX)	07/29/71
Corn	02/15/68	Silver, 1000 oz	07/24/81
Corporate Bond Index	10/28/87	Silver, 5000 oz	08/07/74
Cotton	08/23/72	Swiss Franc	02/13/75
CRB Index	06/12/88	Soybeans	02/02/68
Crude Oil	03/30/83	Soybean Meal	02/06/68
Eurodollar	02/01/82	Soybean Oil	03/04/68
European Curr Unit	01/07/86	Sugar #11	10/04/71
Federal Funds	10/03/88	T-bills	01/06/76
Feeder Cattle	06/03/76	T-bonds	09/21/77
German Mark	02/13/75	T-bonds (day only)	09/21/77
Gold (COMEX)	12/31/74	T-bonds (Midam)	12/10/87
Gold, Kilo	01/07/83	T-note (5 yr)	05/06/87
Heating Oil	05/06/79	T-note (5 yr, CBT)	05/20/88
Japanese Yen	11/03/76	T-note (10 yr)	05/03/82
Liquid Propane	08/21/87	T-note (day only)	05/03/82
Live Cattle	06/23/69	Unleaded Gasoline	12/03/84
Live Hogs	06/25/69	US Dollar Index	11/20/85
Lumber	11/16/72	Value Line Index	02/24/82
Maxi Market Index	08/08/85	Wheat (Chicago)	04/01/68
Mini Value Line	07/29/83	Wheat (Kansas City)	04/09/76
Municipal Bonds	06/11/85	Wheat (Minn spring)	11/18/80
NYFE Stock Index	05/06/82		

Segmenting the Data

Another question that must be resolved is whether to test the data in one piece or in a series of smaller pieces. Testing the data as one big chunk would seem to be statistically sound. However, this approach can mask some important information. Namely, how did it do period by period? A model that makes $100,000 in a 10-year period looks great, but what if it is all based on one or two very good years and the other eight are losses or very marginal performers? Consequently, it is better to test the entire time period as a number of smaller intervals. Five 2-year divisions of a 10-year test are good. If the trading model is more long term and generates too few trades to provide statistical validity in a 2-year period, 3- or 4-year divisions may be more appropriate. This is discussed in more detail in Chapter 7, "Optimizing the Trading System."

Testing

After these questions have been resolved, a basket of markets and a period of history will have been selected. The test basket should follow the suggested group breakdown, and testing should be done on at least 10 years of history per market broken down into five 2-year periods with respect to daily data. This range of history includes a significant selection of different market types and conditions.

The multimarket, multiperiod test uses the same "reasonable" values for the trading model in every market and each time period. The test is simple. The trading model is tested on each of the five time periods in each of the 10 markets in the basket. Performance for each market and each period is tabulated and evaluated.

The specific purpose of this test is to obtain an overview of profit and risk performance. A trading model that is designed to be optimizable at its inception cannot be expected to produce peak performance over many markets and time periods using only one set of "reasonable" model parameters. However, it is expected that a robust and sound model will perform moderately well under such a test spanning a range of markets and historical periods. A model that performs poorly overall should be rejected at this point.

Marginal performance would be a fairly even mix of small profits and small losses over the basket and over the different time segments. If this occurs, the system is questionable. At best, it shows that the model has components that depend on adaptation to particular markets and conditions to achieve performance. This would be indicated by a model that shows good profit in conditions that are appropriate for its style and losses in conditions that are difficult for it. Such a model is worth pursuing further. Such might be the case with a model that shows no connection between performance and market conditions. Such a model should probably be rejected at this level of testing. If there is some plausible reason for this type of behavior, it would be worth taking it to the next level of testing.

If performance shows large losses throughout the basket and history, even if there is an occasional strong showing, the trading system is bad. Abandon ship. Unconditionally.

Performance that shows tremendous profit with low risk throughout the basket and history is very promising. Excellent early results promise profit and are grounds for optimism. Of course, further testing is required.

7

OPTIMIZING THE
TRADING SYSTEM

Once the trading model has passed the multimarket and multiperiod test, it is ready for optimization. The structure of the optimization tests parallels that of the tests presented in the previous chapter; however, these tests differ in one very important way. During optimization, model performance will be calculated at many different values for the key model parameters.

Before the mechanics of optimization are presented, it is necessary to explore the purpose of optimization and its limitations. Recall the definition from the *American Heritage Dictionary* presented in Chapter 2:

Optimize: *To make the most effective use of.*

According to this definition, to *optimize* a trading system is to make the most effective use of it. How does optimization accomplish this? By an empirical examination and evaluation of all potential model variable candidates. Remember, a trading system comprises rules, formulas, and variables. The rules and formulas define the model structure. It might be said that they are its skeleton. The variables breathe life into the system. Perhaps they should be thought of as its lifeblood.

Different values for a trading model can lead to dramatically different profit and risk performance. Ideally, the most robust model will only yield less or more profit with different model values. In practice, with many optimizable trading systems, different parameter sets can mean the difference between profit and loss. This is why proper optimization is so important.

Incorrect optimization can lead to overfitting and other serious errors. If such errors in optimization are overlooked, the resultant trading model will show very good optimization results and very poor real-time trading performance. This is the main reason proper optimization methods are critical to successful trading.

This chapter will present the mechanics of optimization. A thorough grasp of all the issues in Chapter 4 is necessary for an understanding of proper optimization methodology. Chapters 8, 9, and 10 will present helpful, detailed guidelines regarding other important considerations.

OPTIMIZATION

A number of equally valid terms can be used to describe the optimization process: the test batch, test run, variable scan, the estimation process, and so on. In this book, *optimization* will mean *parameter selection*. The goal of optimization is to find the values for model parameters that will generate peak trading performance in real time.

Notice that the emphasis is on peak trading performance and real-time trading. These foci may seem obvious; unfortunately, many practitioners of optimization really are not achieving these goals. Inadvertently, such users of trading software think that the optimization result showing the biggest profit is one and the same as that trading model generating peak real-time trading performance.

This scenario can occur. However, if the optimization uses an insufficient data sample, it will most likely yield too small a sample of trades to be statistically significant. If it is done on an unrepresentative data sample, the model will likely perform poorly when it encounters a different market or trend condition. If the degrees of freedom are restricted by too many conditions, the statistical validity of the results is questionable. If the top model found during optimization is a profit "spike," instead of the top of a gradual round hill, the model will offer little robustness when price patterns shift. If the model has not been walk-forward tested, there can be little confidence in its real-time trading abilities. A model that is the result of careless and incomplete optimization is quite likely to lead to substantial real-time trading losses.

When an optimization is attempted with no regard to the proper statistical guidelines and procedures, it can rapidly degenerate into what has been commonly referred to as "curve fitting." It is common knowledge among statistical modelers that given enough variables, a curve can be made to fit any number of data points. Because a curve produced by modeling procedures fits past data quite closely is no guarantee that it will be a good predictor of future movement. Closeness of fit does not imply the best predictive power. In our work, it is often just the opposite.

When using a statistical method, the model that best fits a large and representative data sample with sufficient degrees of freedom, has robust parameters, and has passed a walk-forward analysis will be the best predictor of future action.

SETTING UP THE OPTIMIZATION FRAMEWORK

Setting up the optimization framework is simple; however, it requires caution and thoroughness (see Figure 7-1). There are five components to the optimization framework: (1) selection of the model parameters and (2) setting of their scan ranges; (3) the size of the data sample must be set; (4) a proper evaluation type must be established to find the best model; (5) evaluation criteria for the entire test run must be selected.

Selecting the Parameters

The model parameters that have the largest impact on performance are the ones to be used in the optimization framework. If a parameter has little impact on performance, there is no reason to make it a candidate for optimization. Instead, a fixed value or *constant* should be used during optimization.

If the relative significances of the model parameters are not known, an extra step is needed to determine their importance. The easiest way to do this is by scanning a relevant range of parameters for each model variable, one at a time. If a scan of a relevant range of parameters shows dramatic change, then it is an important parameter. If, conversely, such a scan shows little or no change on performance, it is an insignificant variable. This also raises the question as to whether this variable has any place at all in the trading model. Based on the results of these preliminary

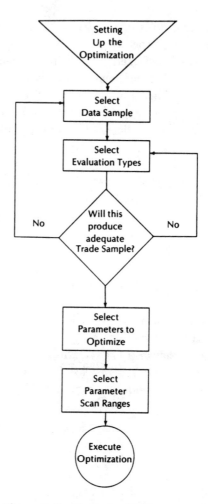

Figure 7-1   Optimization Framework

scans, the value for the insignificant parameters can be fixed or they can be eliminated from the model.

Selecting the Scan Range

Selection of a relevant range for testing a parameter has two guidelines. First, the range should be appropriate for the indicator, rule, or model. In other words, scanning a range of 1 to 1,000 days for a short-term moving average contradicts the idea of short-term (often considered 3 to 10 days) and is way outside the normal range used in moving averages (e.g., 3 to

200 days). A more meaningful scan range would be 1 to 13 days for a short-term moving average.

The computation time dictated by a scan range must be controlled. This becomes particularly relevant when doing multivariable scans. Scanning a range of moving averages from 1 to 13 days in steps of 2 requires only seven tests, which is computationally insignificant no matter how slow the individual tests are. Scanning a range of 1 to 200 in steps of 1 requires 200 tests, more than 28 times as many as the first scan range. It becomes pointless if the parameter has little effect on performance or if the values are outside the normal range.

The size of the step taken in a scan range is significant beyond its demands on computer time. Scanning a variable too closely can do more than consume computer time; it can inadvertently result in curve fitting, especially if proper measures are not taken to protect against the selection of a profit spike instead of a profit hill. Scanning a short-term moving average from 1 to 13 days in steps of 1 day at a time is valid.

Scanning a long-term moving average from 10 to 200 in steps of 1 day will tend to increase the likelihood of curve fitting, decrease the validity of results, and weight the results to the long term. This is because a 5% shift in this average at a length of 100 days leads to averages of 95 or 105. Compare a 5% shift at 20 days, which leads to averages of 19 or 21. Tests at 100 are five times more frequent.

Selecting the Data Sample

Two rules govern the selection of a proper data sample: a size large enough to assure statistical validity, and a scope that includes a sufficiently broad range of market conditions. These factors also have an impact on each other. The size of the test data must be sufficient to generate a statistically significant sample of trades. Ideally this should be at least 30 per sample, and the more the better.

The number of rules "consume" data that restrict the degrees of freedom. Consequently, the size of the data sample and the number of trades generated must be large enough to accommodate the restrictions dictated by both the trading model and by the optimization framework.

Consider the following example. A trading model that uses 2 moving averages is tested on a data sample of 200 days. The longest moving average can be 50 days in length. This calculation uses 50 days of data, thereby "consuming," 50 degrees of freedom. This leaves 150 days which can produce signals. If five trades are generated we have 2 moving averages, a stop-loss, . . . (i.e., 5 rules producing 5 trades). Therefore, this test must either be rejected or modified. It can be modified by expanding the number of data points in the sample, reducing the length of the longest moving average in the test, or eliminating restricting rules.

The second principle can prove more difficult to meet. The data sample should be representative of the market as a whole. It should contain as many types of trends, patterns, and situations as possible: bullish, bearish, congested, and cyclic. It should also contain as many different levels of volatility as possible: high, average, and low.

There are guidelines to follow. Include as much variation in price data as possible and use a sample size that is relevant to the style of the model. This is the rule of the largest and most general possible sample. If this approach proves impractical, get as much data as possible resembling the current market conditions. This is the rule of the most relevant possible sample.

Selecting the Model Evaluation Type

The guidelines for the selection of the evaluation type, objective function, or test criteria have been presented in detail in Chapter 5, "Search and Judgment." At this point in the optimization, a method must be chosen. The objective is to use the evaluation type that will select the most robust model during the optimization process. This may vary depending on demands of different types of trading models.

Selecting the Test Result Evaluation Type

The results of an optimization must also be evaluated. They must first be evaluated for statistical significance. Recall that 1% of all tests will be "highly significant" and 5% of all tests will be statistically "significant." This means that if the top model is found and only 1% or thereabouts of the entire test run is profitable, the top model is probably statistically meaningless and therefore it is not likely to be terribly robust. Similarly, if only 5% of the entire test is marginally profitable, the top model is also likely to be a statistical anomaly and lack robustness.

Therefore, to lend any credibility to the top models found, the mean of all tests must be profitable and one standard deviation below the mean must be profitable. The larger the percentage of very profitable models found in a test batch, the greater the likelihood that this is a sound trading model, unless the test range is narrow. A sound model has many profitable parameter combinations.

The second way to evaluate an optimization run is by the "shape" of the results space. A top model must be rejected if it is a *profit spike,* which is another type of anomaly. The performance of such a model turns from profit to loss at the smallest shift in its parameters. In Figure 7–2, profit sharply rises and falls to a high profit at 75% volatility in a breakout trading system forming an unstable profit spike.

The optimization process must select a top model that is sitting on top of a gently sloping profit "hill." The performance of such a model will only show a small reduction of profit in the face of small-to-medium shifts in parameters. In very robust models, even the most drastic shift may only lead to a large decrease in profit instead of a loss. This translates into stability of real-time performance. The model is likely to perform better than others under a wider variety of future price patterns. In Figure 7–3, profit gradually rises and declines as a function of the percentage of volatility variable in a breakout trading system forming a large stable area.

Summary

A sound optimization must begin by selecting the variables to be included—those that are most significant to the results. Next, the appropriate scan ranges for the selected variables must be determined, keeping them as broad as possible, but distributed to avoid unwanted bias. The proper data sample size must be determined to include as many price patterns and trends as possible. The correct model evaluation type must

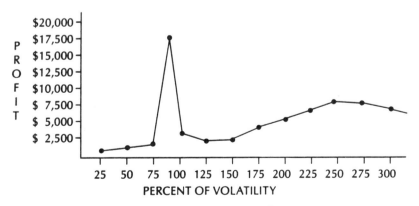

Figure 7–2   Profit Spike

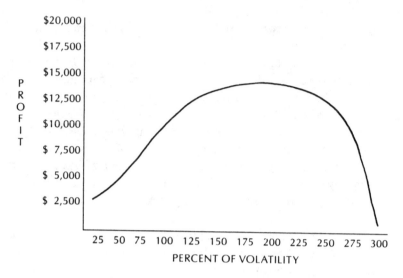

Figure 7-3   Percentage of Volatility

be used to select the most robust model. Finally, the correct test batch evaluation criteria must be used to select the model that is most likely to perform best under real-time conditions. Only when all these steps have been followed can a valid optimization be performed.

A MULTIMARKET AND MULTIPERIOD OPTIMIZATION

The structure of the multimarket, multiperiod optimization parallels that of the multimarket and multiperiod test outlined in the previous chapter. The purpose is to obtain a more precise determination of profit and risk based on the performance of optimal model parameters (see Figure 7-4).

Optimization of the model is done on a diversified basket of markets to obtain a measure of the trading model's versatility and robustness. The more markets that a model can trade, the more useful it is. It is not so obvious that the more markets a model can trade well, the more robust the model. Such broader based testing offers greater statistical validity. There is a further consideration. A trading model that can perform well on a diversified basket of markets is more likely to be based on some more general principle of price action. A model that performs well on only one market, unless that was its specific intention from the beginning, is always suspect.

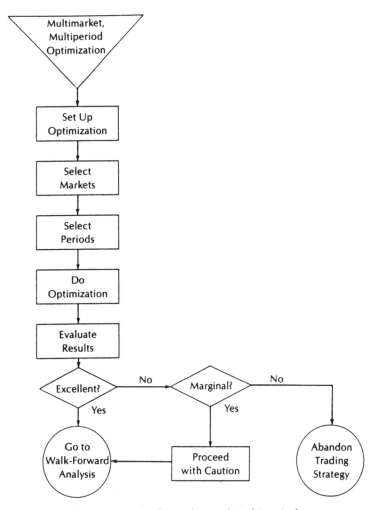

Figure 7-4   Multimarket and Multiperiod

The optimization of the model is also done on a selection of different time periods. Trends change. Volatility changes. Liquidity changes. Fundamental conditions of supply and demand change. Therefore, a model that trades well in a few time periods and poorly in others requires further examination. Was the price action hostile in the periods in which the model performed poorly? If so, the model may still require rethinking. If the price action was reasonable but different, there may be a flaw in design. In a similar way, there can be price action that is extremely friendly to a trading model. In such an environment, the performance of the trading model will prove to be good. As the exception, it cannot be taken as a typical measure of performance.

What will such an optimization test look like? It will look like the following for one market:

Optimize T-bond futures

Scan Moving Average   1 day to 31 days in steps of 2 days
Scan Stop Loss   1 pt to 6 pts in steps of 1 pt

Total number of scans per optimization   96

Do this on price periods: 1981 through 1982
                          1983 through 1984
                          1985 through 1986
                          1987 through 1988
                          1989 through 1990

Total number of scans for 5-period optimization   480

Apply this same 128 scan, 5-historical-period test to the remaining 9 markets in the basket: coffee, cotton, crude oil, gold, pork bellies, soybeans, S&P 500, sugar, and Swiss francs.

Total number of scans for 10-market, 5-period optimization   4,800

How Does the Model Respond to Optimization?

The first step is to see how the trading model responds to optimization. There is always an outside chance that the model parameters chosen a priori in the first test are, in fact, the optimal parameters. This is, however, highly unlikely to be the case for a 10-market, 5-period test. This is one reason for the size and scope of this testing cycle; it should be broad enough to ensure optimal parameters within its bounds.

Average performance during the multimarket and multiperiod optimization should improve over that of the multimarket and multiperiod test. It is unlikely that the randomly chosen value in the first test will generate peak performance. This is particularly apparent with a multi-variable optimization. Often, many synergies exist between multiple variables; the full extent of this synergy, as measured by profit, is generally uncovered by optimization. For these reasons, near peak profit performance should be expected during the multimarket, multiperiod optimization. This is the function of optimization.

For example, assume the average annual profit is $2,000 for a 1-market, 5-period test. It is reasonable to expect a higher average annual profit for a 1-market, 5-period optimization of this market. In addition, a similar improvement in annual profit should occur for each market when it is optimized.

The performance of all the tests in each of the individual optimizations should be viewed as a batch and should meet statistical criteria required to validate these results. At least 30% of all tests per optimization should equal or exceed predetermined minimum profitability thresholds based on broad-range tests. A higher percentage of profitable models per optimization points to a more robust trading model. A very low percentage of profitable models may be little more than a profit spike and a statistical anomaly of little or no predictive value.

There should be evidence that the selected top model is surrounded by other good performers and is therefore not an isolated profit spike. Each optimization should have a large enough data sample and a group of variable scan ranges that ensure a statistically sound number of degrees of freedom. Each optimization should be designed to produce a statistically valid number of trades. Trading performance must meet the essential criteria of even distribution throughout the data sample.

What Is Better Performance?

Better performance is evaluated in three dimensions. An increase in the annualized rate of return is dear to the primary motive of trading. Increased profit is an estimation of the dollars per invested capital unit that can be anticipated. However, to the experienced trader, a decrease or stabilization of annualized risk as measured by maximum drawdown is equally desirable. A decrease in risk reduces required trading capital. This translates directly into increased yield without an increase in risk.

The percentage of winning trades is another important measure of improvement. A more accurate trading model can sometimes translate into a larger average trade. It also adds a great deal to a trader's "comfort zone." A greater feeling of comfort leads to greater confidence in a model. This results in a willingness to follow the trading system and to not second-guess it.

Average annualized trading performance should now be at an acceptable level when judged by standard investment criteria. Each trader must determine an acceptable rate of profit for the level of risk that is part of his or her trading strategy.

For example, $10,000 invested in a T-bill may generate a 5% yield with no risk of capital loss. This is not a high yield, but it must be viewed as a "risk-free" investment. In contrast, $10,000 traded in futures runs a risk of capital loss. These losses can be very large, and there is a chance that they may exceed the original investment.

Because the risk of leveraged futures trading is so high, trading yields must be well above those of other less risky investments. A 10% annualized yield on trading capital would be unacceptable in the eyes of many traders. With proper trading system design and testing, risk can be reasonably estimated as a percentage of trading capital. However, because of the high leverage and the nature of economic price shocks, a complete loss of trading capital can never be ruled out. A small chance of a loss exceeding capitalization always exists, even though it may never appear in the test results.

The Decision Matrix

If the average profit performance of the system is negative, then it is bad. No further testing is required. Return to the design stage. If upon reevaluation, however, it is determined that the variable scan ranges were too narrow to evaluate performance properly, set them correctly and repeat the multiperiod, multimarket optimization.

If both peak and average performance are still marginal, it is a questionable system and probably of little value. Every optimization test is likely to produce at least a small percentage of profitable and marginally profitable test results. This is why it is essential to judge both peak model performance and the mean performance of the optimization. In all likelihood further testing would probably isolate only an island of good results. Return to the design stage.

If average performance of the trading system is profitable, has acceptable risk, and compares favorably with other investment possibilities, it is excellent. The trading system must now be put to the final and decisive test: the walk-forward analysis. Proceed to the final test.

THE WALK-FORWARD TEST

What is a walk-forward test? It is a two-step process. The first step consists of a traditional optimization as described in the previous sections. The trading model undergoes a scan of parameters. Parameter values are found for the top model, not judged by profit alone. It is the second step that distinguishes the walk forward and is the source of its unusual attributes.

This step is a measure of postoptimization performance. The performance of the parameter values of the "best" model found in the first step, as determined by the objective function, are tested on an additional, adjacent portion of price history. In other words, the top model is tested in a simulation of real-time trading.

To recap, a walk-forward test has two steps. The trading model is first optimized on a piece of history. Then it is "traded" on a new piece of history. This type of testing is also known as *out-of-sample testing* or *double-blind testing.* The walk-forward test is the only method that provides an exact picture of postoptimization trading performance.

The Purpose of the Walk-Forward Test

The walk-forward test has three major purposes. The first two are essential to the completion of a successful test and optimization cycle. The third provides unique and highly useful information that enables reasonably accurate expectation measures of profit and risk in real-time trading.

The primary goal of the walk-forward test is to determine if the performance of a trading model under optimization is real or the result of curve fitting. The performance of the trading model is considered to be "real" if it has predictive value or can effectively react to unseen market movement. It is also a method of determining which parameters will work in the future. The model may be good, but the correct parameters may not always turn up. In a properly designed model, such a quality should result in real-time trading profits in some way commensurate with that uncovered during optimization. If the trading model is going to work in real-time trading, it must first pass a walk-forward test.

The second goal of the walk-forward test is to determine the quality of the actual optimization process. Evidence suggests that even a sound model can be overfit. This can be done by restricting the degrees of freedom with too many rules, using a data sample that is too small, scanning too many variables, or scanning a variable in too fine a step.

The walk-forward test produces a unique performance measure called *walk-forward efficiency.* This measure compares the annualized rate of postoptimization profit with that of in-sample optimization profit. The section "What Rate of Profit Should We Expect?" in this chapter shows how to calculate walk-forward efficiency.

A model is overfit if it has a low walk-forward efficiency; in other words, the walk-forward results are clearly lower than the in-sample test.

The solution to this problem is to diagnose and eliminate one of the four causes of overfitting listed earlier.

If the low walk-forward efficiency is not attributable to a clear-cut abuse that can be repaired, the model must be judged as is. If the trading model offers a lower-grade walk-forward efficiency, the trader must either reject it or be prepared to accept this level of performance.

This leads to the third goal of the walk-forward test: measurement of the profit and risk performance to determine real-time trading expectation. An ideally designed and optimized trading model will profit at a similar rate in out-of-sample or postoptimization trading as it does during in-sample or optimization testing. If it performs significantly worse in the out-of-sample testing, it can be a sign of overfitting. A sound trading model may exceed optimization performance if postoptimization market conditions offer greater profit potential than those in optimization.

Setting Up a Walk-Forward Test

A single walk-forward test is a two-step process: The first step is optimization; the second step is the test of the parameter values of the top model. A walk-forward test requires the variable scan ranges, the size of the optimization window, and the size of the trading or test window.

The length of the optimization window is determined by:

- The availability of data.
- The type of trading system.
- The pace of trading.
- The relevancy of the data.
- The longevity of the optimization.

Furthermore, the length of the optimization window can be estimated empirically by setting up a group of test walk-forward analyses using different-size optimization windows.

Other factors affect how long a model can be traded before reoptimization or how large the trading or test window should be. They are volatility continuity, swing continuity, the violence and frequency of trend changes, and model integrity.

In theory, if market conditions never varied from those found in the optimization window, the model would never require reoptimization. In practice, however, a model tested on two years of data may be tradable for three to six months. A model built on one year of data may last for one to two months. A model built on six months of data may last for two to four weeks. The walk-forward trading window should be approximately 10% to 20% of the optimization window.

An Example of a Walk-Forward Test

To illustrate, consider the following example of a 2-variable scan done with a trading system called *Blast*, on a 48-month optimization window of S&P 500 futures price data:

Price History	:	S&P 500 futures
Optimization Window Size	:	48 months
Historical Period	:	7/1/82–6/30/86
Buy Variable	:	Scan 0 to 300 in steps of 20
Sell Variable	:	Scan 0 to 300 in steps of 20

This first step of the walk-forward test does a standard optimization scan of two key model variables on S&P price data from 7/1/82 to 6/30/86. The computer will then review the 256 model candidates specified by this 2-variable scan. The evaluation criteria will select a top model. This is a standard optimization.

The second step in the walk-forward test assesses the postoptimization performance of the top model found in the first step. This step adds a new piece of historical data, called the "trading window" or "test window" to that of the optimization window data. The model parameters of the top model are tested on this piece of data. In other words, the top model is evaluated or traded on price data that were not part of the original optimization data. This test will look as follows:

Price History	:	S&P 500 futures
Trading Window	:	6 months
Historical Period Traded	:	7/1/86–12/31/86
Optimization P&L	:	$47,390
Annual Optimization P&L	:	$11,847
Optimization Drawdown	:	$6,175
Trading P&L	:	$20,265
Annual Trading P&L	:	$40,530
Walk-Forward Efficiency	:	341%

In the example, a top model is found by using optimization on a 48-month period of history and is then traded forward or tested on a 6-month period of history immediately following the 48-month optimization period. The top model made $47,390 during its 48-month optimization test, an annualized profit of $11,847. It made $20,265 during its 6-month postoptimization test, an annualized profit of $40,530.

This is impressive. Still, one successful walk-forward test can be a product of chance therefore it is essential to conduct a more comprehensive test called a *walk-forward analysis*. A walk-forward analysis is a series of individual walk-forward tests. To be statistically reliable, it must consist of a sufficiently large number of tests.

THE WALK-FORWARD ANALYSIS

A walk-forward analysis is a series of individual walk-forward tests over a comprehensive and representative segment of price history (see Figure 7–5). The walk-forward analysis simulates the way that an optimizable trading system is intended to be traded. In the parlance, the method "walks forward" the optimization and trading windows a fixed number of

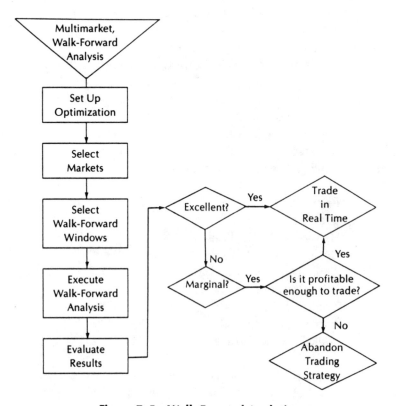

Figure 7–5 Walk-Forward Analysis

time units. The "step window" is the name of this number. The first step in the procedure is a single walk-forward test on the first segment of price history. The next step in the procedure is another walk-forward test on the next segment of price history. This process is then repeated until the period of history to be traded has been completed.

In the walk-forward analysis test, the evaluation of the trading model exclusively on the basis of postoptimization performance is one of the most dramatic departures from other forms of testing. The walk-forward analysis judges the performance and tradability of the trading system on postoptimization versus optimization performance. The composite results of many optimizations are used for comparison. A model would be rejected on the basis of a walk-forward analysis that was unprofitable or that showed great numbers in optimization and very poor numbers in the walk-forward.

The Purpose of the Walk-Forward Analysis

The primary purpose of the walk-forward analysis is to prove the validity of the trading model and the optimization procedure beyond reasonable doubt. It extends the benefits of the walk-forward test to a large enough sample of data and walk-forward tests to provide statistical rigor. The walk-forward analysis is designed to do a large enough number of walk-forward tests to overcome random results. A test including at least 10 walk-forward tests approaches such reliability.

The second purpose of the walk-forward analysis is to arrive at a more accurate picture of the profit and risk profile based on a larger and more statistically valid sample. This analysis consists of multiple optimizations and multiple walk-forward tests. These are batched together to provide a more reliable measure of performance.

In addition, a comparison of the postoptimization performance with that of optimization performance provides a more realistic and reliable estimation of future profit. Assume it is now time to begin to trade the model in real time. It is known from testing that the trading model has walked forward at a pace equal to 75% of that of optimization. The optimization for the most current data has produced a $20,000 profit per year. The WFE (walk-forward efficiency) of 75% indicates that the model should profit somewhere in an area equal to 75% of $20,000 per year, or $15,000 a year. This is helpful in evaluating the real-time performance of the model.

The walk-forward analysis provides much greater insight into maximum drawdown than any other testing measure. A real problem with taking the maximum drawdown found in optimization as a measure of future drawdowns stems from the nature of the optimization process itself. Most models with large drawdowns will be rejected during optimization. The drawdowns uncovered during the walk-forward analysis test have the same validity as do postoptimization profits. They are what happens after optimization when a model encounters some more volatile, less predictable price movement. The drawdown found in the walk-forward analysis test is, once again, based on a much larger sample of such tests.

The third purpose of the walk-forward analysis test is to verify the optimization process itself. As mentioned earlier, an unsound model will simply flunk the walk-forward analysis test. However, a sound model can be overfit or violate other principles and perform poorly on the walk-forward analysis test for "technical reasons." Considerations such as degrees of freedom, optimization and test window size, the range and fineness of the variable scan, and the number of variables scanned enter into this evaluation. The best model fits "loosely" and has lots of profitable neighbors. The worst model fits too "tightly" and stands alone on a pinnacle of atypical profit. The walk-forward analysis test defends against these errors of optimization.

The walk-forward analysis is a rigorous simulation of the way in which an optimizable trading system is most often used in real-time trading. An important question among users of optimizable software is how often the trading system should be reoptimized. The fourth goal of the walk-forward analysis test is to answer this question. The test provides this answer in the best way possible: empirically.

If a system achieves peak performance when it is adapted using optimization to current market conditions, then it will need to be reoptimized at some point. Market conditions change. The trading model must change also. This raises the question "when should it be reoptimized?" The use of a model developed with the walk-forward analysis test should mirror the test structure. If the test window is three months, then at the end of every three months of trading, the model must be reoptimized, and so on for different test window sizes.

The fifth goal of the walk-forward analysis test provides a unique and powerful insight into performance. Trading models often have their worst drawdowns when trends or market conditions change. The rolling windows of the walk-forward analysis test show exactly what happens when the selected model meets a condition for which it was not tested. It is in the nature of robust trading models that whereas such a change might cause losses, they should not be terminal. Such effects will be masked by traditional optimization. They are revealed by the walk-forward analysis test.

Recap

The walk-forward analysis provides a valuable source of information and detail. It produces and evaluates three levels of model performance. On the first level, it judges the reward, risk, and trade distribution of a model optimized on one segment of historical data. This is the traditional way that traders judge models. Level One evaluation is sound insofar as it goes; however, it suffers from a lack of verification of post-optimization performance.

The second level of model evaluation is the walk-forward test. This level verifies both the model and the testing process. It also provides a comparison of optimization and postoptimization trading performance. These two essential pieces of information are not provided by Level One. Although a great deal more is known than at the first level, there is still reasonable doubt; the results of one walk-forward test are inconclusive.

In the third level of model evaluation, the walk-forward analysis, the model is judged exclusively on the collective postoptimization trading performance of a series of individual walk-forward tests. One great strength of this level of testing is the statistical significance that comes from its exhaustiveness and scope. Another benefit is the insight it offers regarding the effect of changing trends and volatility on performance.

An Example of a Walk-Forward Analysis

To illustrate, consider a walk-forward analysis that consists of 9 individual walk-forward tests. This analysis will provide the optimization performance of the trading model for 9 different periods of contiguous history. The reward, risk, and internal soundness of each are evaluated. This analysis alone gives us 9 times the information contained in a Level One evaluation.

The analysis will also provide postoptimization performance results on each of the 9 individual walk-forward tests. In other words, it provides 9 tests of postoptimization trading. It also provides performance measures of this postoptimization trading. At this point, there is at least 18 times the information of a Level One evaluation and 9 times the information of a Level Two evaluation. In addition, the walk-forward analysis covers a historical time span that included many different trend and volatility changes. This provides insight into the stability of the trading model with respect to changing market conditions.

Consider an example of an actual walk-forward analysis done by the software trading system *Blast.** The walk-forward analysis details are as follows:

Price History	:	S&P Futures
Historical Period	:	7/1/82–12/24/90
Estimation Window Size	:	48 months
Test Window Size	:	6 months
Step Window Size	:	6 months
Buy Variable	:	Scan 0 to 300 in steps of 20
Sell Variable	:	Scan 0 to 300 in steps of 20
Top Model Comparison	:	Pessimistic return on margin
Top Model Floor One	:	Net profit and loss above $5,000
Top Model Floor Two	:	Risk/reward ratio above 2.0

The walk-forward analysis proceeds as follows. *Blast* loads the S&P 500 futures price data for the first optimization window from 1/2/83 to 6/30/86. It then performs an optimization using the two chosen variables. *Blast* records the top model, that is, the model having the best pessimistic return on margin with a net profit and loss above $5,000 and a risk/reward ratio above 2 (if one exists). It then walks forward this top model. This means that the top model variables are applied to the test window data (7/1/86–12/31/86). These results are tabulated before proceeding to the next optimization window. *Blast* also records the absence of a top model, in which case the test period is not traded and testing proceeds directly to the next optimization window. The walk-forward process continues one step at a time over all the specified historical data. The Walk Forward Net Profit and Loss Summary reports the results of the walk-forward analysis, as shown in Table 7–1.

The numbers in the "Net Profit & Loss" column under the "Optimization Performance" section represent profits for a 4-year optimization period. The numbers in the "Net Profit & Loss" column under the "Walk Forward" section represent profits for a 6-month postoptimization trading period. To determine the numbers under the "WFE"

---

* © Copyright Robert Pardo, available from the Pardo Corporation.

Table 7–1   S&P Futures—7/1/86 to 12/24/90

		Estimation Performance			Walk Forward	
From	To	Net Profit & Loss	Maximum Draw Down	R/R Ratio	Net Profit & Loss	WFE
07/82	06/86	$ 47,390	$ 6,175	7.7	$ 20,265	342%
01/83	12/86	48,440	7,510	6.5	8,750	144
07/83	06/87	55,145	7,510	7.3	9,410	137
01/84	12/87	85,615	9,405	9.1	8,960	84
07/84	06/88	81,870	9,405	8.7	11,715	114
01/85	12/88	81,435	9,405	8.7	8,580	84
07/85	06/89	101,665	16,865	6.0	11,250	89
01/86	12/89	106,640	16,865	6.3	33,450	251
07/86	06/90	145,840	11,555	12.6	38,725	212
Total Profit & Loss					$151,105	
Largest		$145,840	$16,865	12.6	$ 20,265	342%
Smallest		47,390	6,175	6.0	8,580	84
Average		83,782	10,521	8.1	16,789	162

column, the profits in these two columns were first annualized. For example, ($20,265/.5)/($47,390/4) = 342%.

Is the Model Robust?

An examination of the results will determine the robustness of the model. Consider the first line in Table 7–1. Starting with Row 1, the top model found in optimization window 1 (07/82–06/86) produced a profit of $47,390, a drawdown of $6,175 and a reward/risk ratio of 7.7 ($47,390/$6,175 = 7.7). These are good numbers based on an internal examination of an optimization, but more is needed.

How did this particular model work in the walk-forward analysis? The walk-forward profit & loss column for Row 1 shows a profit of $20,265. This is the profit made by the top model in the first 6 months of postoptimization trading (7/86 to 12/86) following the 48-month optimization window. Once again, a good result. But it could still be a lucky result.

Each line in this table presents the same information for 8 additional optimizations and 8 additional walk-forward tests covering 4 more years of trading. All 9 of these postoptimization trading results proved profitable. The total net profit is $151,105. The trading model made money in 100% of the postoptimization test windows. This is a convincing result.

Most importantly, this trading model worked. What does "work" mean in this context? It means that this model made money on data it had never seen. It also means that the model made money during 9 consecutive 6-month periods of unprecedented volatility and change. The model can be considered robust.

What Rate of Profit Should We Expect?

As mentioned in previous sections, walk-forward efficiency (WFE) measures postoptimization against optimization performance. WFE is the ratio of average annualized walk-forward net profit and loss to the average annualized optimization net profit and loss.

It is calculated as follows. The average annualized profit and loss for the nine 48-month optimization periods is $20,945 ($745,040/36 years = $20,945). On average, this model produced a profit of $20,945 per year during optimization.

The average annualized profit for the nine 6-month walk-forward periods is $33,579 ($151,105/4.5 years = $33,579). On average, this model made walk-forward, or postoptimization, profits equal to 160% ($33,579/$20,945 = 160%) of optimization profits. In other words, if a model produces $10,000 per year in profits during optimization, it can be expected to make approximately $16,000 ($10,000 × 1.6 = $16,000) in real-time annualized profits.

What Is the Risk?

The average maximum drawdown during optimization was $10,521 with a high of $16,865 and a low of $6,175. Experience has shown that a model that generates a postoptimization drawdown exceeding 150% of optimization drawdown is showing signs of trouble. Therefore, one measure of risk is the average optimization drawdown times 1.5, or $15,782. This number is more significant because it is based on nine different optimizations covering nine different periods of history.

A second and perhaps even more meaningful measure of risk is provided by a review of the risk/reward ratios of the optimization windows. This shows an average reward/risk ratio of 8.1, the largest at 12.6 and the smallest at 6.0.

Summary

In summary, the walk-forward test is the only known way to find:

- The likelihood of postoptimization profit.
- The rate at which the model will make money postoptimization.
- Postoptimization risk.

The walk-forward analysis is a precise and accurate simulation of the way in which a trader uses the software in real-time trading. As such, the walk-forward analysis transcends testing and becomes the more important part of the trading system, telling you when to and when not to trade.

Evaluating the Walk-Forward Analysis

The structure and benefits of the walk-forward analysis are clear. All that remains is to apply the same rigorous and exhaustive test to the remaining nine markets in the test basket. After this is done, the composite results can be evaluated.

If the walk-forward analysis is unprofitable across the full set of tests, the structure of the test should be evaluated for error. If such error is found, correct the deficiency and repeat the walk-forward analysis. If no such error is found, reject this model. Previous success is attributable to optimization. It is not a robust model.

If the walk-forward analysis is marginally profitable, the structure of the test should be evaluated for error. If such error is found, correct the deficiency and repeat the walk-forward analysis. If no such error is found, the marginal performance is attributable to a modest trading model. Its value may be in its attributes within the context of a larger portfolio.

If the walk-forward analysis is clearly profitable over the entire basket of markets, it is a very sound model. It has passed the most rigorous testing process known. The trader can now use it with confidence yet still with eyes wide open.

8

THE EVALUATION
OF PERFORMANCE

At this point, it is known that the trading model:

- Is built according to specification.
- Is performing in accordance with theoretical expectation.
- Is robust enough to pass the multimarket, multiperiod test.
- Improves with optimization.
- Has passed a multimarket, multiperiod walk-forward analysis.

It is now time to evaluate this robust and promising trading model as an investment by reviewing its internal structure.

THE TRADING MODEL AS AN INVESTMENT

Given the arduous mental process needed to develop a trading model, it is easy to forget that it must compete with other investment vehicles for the use of dollars. Once the trading model has come this far, it may be difficult to abandon even if it is not as good as the competition. The purpose of this chapter is to put the trading model into perspective with the competition.

The Dimension of Risk in Futures Trading

It is important to keep in mind that, on the extreme end of the risk curve, the risk of trading futures is almost unlimited. Futures are highly leveraged. The owner of a futures account is liable for any deficits that occur in the account beyond the money on deposit. In today's markets with their very high overnight volatility, overnight risk can be devastating. Recall the 20-point close-to-open drop in S&P 500 futures on October 19, 1987. For starters, overnight longs sustained a $10,000 loss per contract on the open of this unusual day. In retrospect, the 19th and 20th were uncommon "statistical outliers." They did occur, however, and they did cause both profits and losses of unusual proportion in many traders' accounts.

In markets that have daily limits, overnight risk is still not limited. Daily limits in the face of market-wrenching news can produce a number of locked-limit days. The effect of this can be severe financially and even worse psychologically.

The yield of a trading model must be evaluated in light of the potentially exceptional risk incurred by futures trading. Accordingly, the yield must be substantial enough to justify this extreme yet unlikely risk of the loss of all (plus more) trading capital. The risk must be well defined, thoroughly understood, and acceptable in light of yield. Stringent money management principles must be applied on top of all this to further defend against catastrophic loss. A futures trader cannot be too careful.

Compare the Model to the Alternatives

Ultimately, a trading model competes with virtually risk-free, low-yielding investments such as T-bills, certificates of deposit, money market accounts, and savings accounts.

It may seem absurd to think that a futures trading model might offer such a low yield. However, an inspection of the performance of a number of commodity trading advisors and funds will show that some don't even do this well. Because futures trading is very risky, yields must be high enough to make this risk worth taking.

The trading model must also be compared with alternatives for the investment dollar such as stocks, bonds, real-estate, and art. Successful investment in other areas requires another form of expertise. Yet the trading model must perform in a way that is competitive with them.

In addition, performance must be compared with that of available trading advisors and futures funds. The trading model must be compared with other available trading models.

The expense of maintenance, especially the time needed to support the program, must also be considered as a cost of doing business. If a trading model requires hours of maintenance per week, the yield, to justify such an effort, must be sufficiently higher than other trading models that require less time.

In short, the profit and risk profile of a trading model must be superior to any other form of available investment opportunities or offer valuable diversification. In addition, the yield of the model must justify its cost of doing business. Finally, the psychology of the trader must be compatible with the performance profile of the trading model.

THE EVALUATION OF RISK

All business is done at a cost. The cost of trading profit is defined by two things: risk and margin. These sections detail the assessment of profit within the context of risk and cost.

It is generally accepted that the single most important measure of risk in a trading model is maximum drawdown. There are, however, some differences of opinion on the definition of maximum drawdown.

- *Maximum drawdown* is the dollar value of the larger of either the largest series of consecutive losing trades or the largest single loss.
- *Maximum equity drawdown* is the value of the largest dip in the equity curve before a new high point is reached in a trading account.

Maximum drawdown can include both losing and winning trades.

Maximum drawdown has a number of points of interest. To a very large degree, the psychological make up of most traders is highly resistant to long losing streaks, even if they are not particularly large in dollars. Trading is about making money. To many traders, however, trading is also about being right. Losing streaks damage the ego of such traders. Therefore, a full appreciation of the scope of the losing streak is essential. If the trader is not psychologically prepared to accept a typical drawdown of this sort, it may prove difficult to stick by the trading model when it enters such a period in real-time trading.

REQUIRED CAPITAL

Required capital is the amount of money it is expected to take to trade a model successfully. Now that risk is defined, required capital can be intelligently discussed. Required capital consists of margin plus risk.

To trade a futures contract, a trader must deposit initial margin. These rates are set by the exchanges and the clearing firm. They change from time to time based on the volatility of the market and occasionally because of regulation. The first component of required capital is enough money to have the initial margin when a trade is assumed.

The second component of required capital is to have enough invested to cover risk as measured by maximum equity drawdown. It is essential to trading success that an account is able to sustain such a drawdown and still be in a position to continue trading.

Therefore, at minimum, a trading account would require initial margin plus a dollar amount equal to maximum equity drawdown. Assume initial margin of $10,000 and a maximum equity drawdown of $15,000:

Minimum required capital = $10,000 + $15,000
Minimum required capital = $25,000

This minimum capital of $25,000 can sustain a $15,000 drawdown and afford one more trade. It must be profitable. If it is a loss, the account no longer has initial margin and can no longer trade. The prudent trader hopes for the best and prepares for the worst. The worst can be a drawdown larger than that previously experienced.

Therefore, the prudent trader will invest sufficient trading capital to accommodate maximum equity drawdown and leave enough to continue trading. Consider required capital, if maximum equity drawdown is $15,000, and an allowance is made for a future drawdown of $30,000:

Maximum drawdown plus 100% = $15,000 × 2.0
Minimum required capital   = $10,000 + $30,000
Minimum required capital   = $40,000

Some professional traders protect themselves from maximum drawdowns equal to three times the expected. The required capital will be:

Maximum drawdown times 3   = $15,000 × 3.0
Minimum required capital   = $10,000 + $45,000
Minimum required capital   = $55,000

The prudent trader can also make allowances for the worst in another way. Required capital will leave a margin plus a buffer after maximum equity drawdown. In other words, assume the required margin is equal to margin plus a percentage. Incorporating this additional caution into the previous example, required capital will be:

Maximum drawdown times 3	= $10,000 × 3
Initial margin times 1.5	= $5,000 × 1.5
Minimum required capital	= $7,500 + $30,000
Minimum required capital	= $42,500

With these allowances for maximum prudence with respect to both initial margin and maximum drawdown, required capital now is $42,500 versus the first required capital of $15,000 with no safety buffers. Since studies have shown that undercapitalization, or overtrading, is one of the primary causes of loss among traders, it is most prudent to seek out the correct required capital before trading a model.

THE EVALUATION OF PROFIT

After net profit and annualized profit of the trading model have compared favorably with other investment alternatives, they must next be judged with reference to the model's two costs: risk and required capital. Profit cannot be judged in isolation.

An annualized profit of $10,000 sounds great. If it requires $200,000 to obtain it, there is a 5% per annum return on investment. This doesn't sound as great. If the risk is 25% of capital, or $50,000, which represents a reward-to-risk ratio of 1 to 4, it sounds worse yet.

Conversely, the same annual profit of $10,000 takes on a more appealing cast if it requires $5,000 in capital, with a risk of 20%, or $1,000. This translates into a 200% yield on capital with a reward-to-risk ration of 5 to 1.

The Reward-to-Risk Ratio

These examples make clear that the assessment of profit must be performed in comparison with the risk that must be endured to achieve it. The reward-to-risk ratio (RRR) is such a measure; it compares maximum reward represented by annualized profit with maximum risk represented by maximum drawdown. In other words,

Reward/Risk Ratio = Annualized Profit/Maximum Drawdown

For example, an annualized profit of $25,000 divided by a maximum drawdown of $5,000 yields a reward-to-risk ratio of 5.0.

Reward/Risk Ratio = Annualized Profit/Maximum Drawdown
Reward/Risk Ratio = $25,000/$5,000
Reward/Risk Ratio = 5.0

As a rule, the bigger the reward-to-risk ratio the better. A bigger RRR implies that the reward per trading dollar is increasing relative to the risk per trading dollar. Many trading models offer RRRs of 5:1 and 10:1. It must be noted, however, that the validity of this number is in direct proportion to the statistical validity of its components, net profit and maximum drawdown.

Return on Capital

The examples cited indicate that profit must be judged as a return on investment. The determination of required capital will be discussed in detail later in this chapter. For now, it will be taken as how much money is needed to trade a model. The calculation of return on capital is simple. Annualized profit is divided by minimum required capital. Required capital is the sum of margin plus maximum drawdown multiplied by a safety factor. (See discussion on pp. 150–151.)

$$\text{Annualized profit} = \$25,000$$
$$\text{Required capital} \;\; = \$35,000$$
$$\text{Return on capital} = \$25,000/\$35,000$$
$$= 71.4\% \text{ per annum}$$

The benefit of viewing the yield on an annualized basis is the ease of comparison. Most investments are conventionally shown in terms of annual yield. It also makes it easy to compare this performance with other trading models. As will be seen when required capital is defined, such a performance measure is the most realistic way to judge a trading model.

Model Efficiency

Another way in which profit must be compared is within the context of what the market is offering. Markets offer more or less profit potential at different times. When they are "hot" (i.e., trending with high volatility), profit potential can be very high. When they are "cold" (i.e., nontrending with low volatility), profit potential can be very low.

The measurement of the potential profit that a market offers is not a widely understood idea. *Potential profit* is the profit that could be realized by buying every bottom and selling every top. More precisely, it is the sum of every price change where each change is taken as a positive number. It is an excellent way to judge model performance. It must not be expected that a trading model will squeeze every last penny out of a market.

An excellent measure of model performance is the efficiency with which the trading model converts potential profits offered by the market into trading profits. This measure is simple to calculate: Divide the net trading profit by the potential market profit.

For example, assume a net profit of $25,000 and a potential market profit of $300,000 (long at every bottom and short at every top):

$$\text{Model efficiency} = (\$25,000/\$300,000) \times 100$$
$$= 8.33\%$$

This is actually quite good. Experience has shown that trading models with model efficiencies of 5% and better are good based on closing prices. This percentage will decline when tested with intraday ticks.

The model efficiency measure makes it easy to compare market-to-market performance and to evaluate model performance on a year-to-year basis. Markets change. They get hot and potential profit rises. They get cold and potential profit falls. Viewed solely in light of profit, such variation from year to year is difficult to judge. However, model efficiency that remains rather stable year after year indicates a good, robust model. It continues to extract a similar percentage of potential profit even as it waxes and wanes.

TRADING CONSISTENCY

Consistency in trading is the most essential characteristic of a robust trading model. Although this may sound complicated, it really is not. The more consistent the trading model in every way, the better. Conversely, the more erratic and inconsistent, the less robust and, consequently, the more suspect the trading model.

The Distribution of Profit and Loss

The evenness of the distribution of profit and loss throughout the test sample is a major measure of consistency. Net profit alone tells nothing of its distribution; the distribution of profit and loss is a more important consideration. A good distribution is evidence of a robust and consistent model, whereas a poor distribution calls into question the validity of the model.

Assume that a trading model has a walk-forward profit of $50,000 with a maximum drawdown of $10,000 over the five years 1986 through 1990. This profit and risk look excellent.

Three different cases of profit distribution will illustrate the significance of this measure. In the first case, assume the following distribution of profit and loss:

Year	Profit	Drawdown
1986	$50,000	$ 5,000
1987	30,000	6,000
1988	10,000	7,000
1989	(15,000)	9,000
1990	(25,000)	10,000
Total	$50,000	

A glance at the distribution of profit and loss on a year-by-year basis gives pause. Why? The biggest profit was made in the most distant year. The biggest loss was made in the most recent year. In addition, the direction of year-by-year profit and loss is on a clear, downward slope from the most distant past to the most recent past, a bad sign. To make matters worse, the year-by-year drawdowns are in a clear uptrend from the most distant to the most recent past, another bad sign. Furthermore, the variance of the profits and losses is erratic.

The conclusion that can be drawn is that this trading model prospered greatly in 1986. Its profit was large enough to mask a poor performance in 1989 and 1990. This model enjoyed great prosperity in 1986, experienced declining prosperity in 1987 and 1988, and ran into bad times in 1989 and 1990. The model may be flawed, or these past two years may just have been very bad for it. Seemingly, the market has been changing in a manner that is incompatible with the model. But the real question is "How will it do in 1991?" This, of course, can only be answered by guessing whether 1991 will be more like 1986 or 1990.

Consider a second case with the following distribution:

Year	Profit	Drawdown
1986	($ 15,000)	$ 5,000
1987	110,000	10,000
1988	(15,000)	7,000
1989	(15,000)	6,000
1990	(15,000)	4,000
Total	$ 50,000	

Even a cursory inspection will lead to outright rejection of this trading model. Its net profit of $50,000 is based on $110,000 of profit in 1987, the only profitable year. Every other year has a consistent loss of $15,000. The large net profit in 1987 masks a host of worry in every other year. The validity of this model is questionable. Certainly, it requires reevaluation and is not tradable as it currently exists. It must be rejected.

Consider the third case with the following distribution:

Year	Profit	Drawdown
1986	$10,000	$10,000
1987	5,000	3,000
1988	10,000	4,000
1989	10,000	5,000
1990	15,000	4,000
Total	$50,000	

This even distribution through all five years of trading reinforces confidence in the profit of $50,000 and drawdown of $10,000. In addition, the model shows a favorable upward direction in profit from the more distant to recent data. It also shows a favorable downward tendency in drawdown from past to present. The variance of the profits is small as is the variance of drawdowns, with the exception of that in 1986. Furthermore, this model had its worst drawdown in the most distant past. All of this adds up to a very satisfying and acceptable model that is thriving in the most recent test period.

Consider the last case with the following distribution:

Year	Profit	Drawdown
1986	($25,000)	$10,000
1987	(15,000)	9,000
1988	10,000	7,000
1989	30,000	6,000
1990	50,000	5,000
Total	$50,000	

This case is the inverse of the first case. It has the same questionable uneven distribution of profit and loss. However, it has two very desirable features. It has a positive upward sloping direction of profit from 1986 to 1990. It also has a favorable decline in drawdowns from 1986 forward. Furthermore, it is positively thriving in 1990 with its best performance in every category.

The question that must be answered is "Why?" If this model is to be traded, a sound explanation of these "trends" in year-to-year profit and loss must be made. Is the trading strategy better able to operate under conditions that have been changing? One explanation would be very congested and trendless activity in 1986 and 1987 contrasted with a strong clean trend and rising volatility starting in 1988 and progressing forward.

The evaluation of the distribution of profits, losses, and drawdowns follows simple rules. The more even the distribution, the better. The more distant the acceptable maximum drawdown, the better. No one time period should be disproportionately responsible for the overall profit.

If there is a direction to profit, it should be up. Conversely, if there is a trajectory to drawdown, it should be down. Any clear-cut trend of profit or risk must also be noted. Just as trends change in markets, so can "trends" in trading model profit and risk.

The Distribution of Trades

The distribution of trades is usually calculated in the same manner as that of the distribution of profit and loss per time period. The more consistent and even the distribution, the better.

The best trading system is one with profits as well as losses distributed evenly throughout the test period. Evenness of distribution through out the testing period is characteristic of a robust and stable trading model. The distribution of wins and losses will never be so even as to allow for the prediction of the next profit or loss. It is also important to reject any trading system that has more than 50% of its overall profit attributable to one trade.

The next step in the evaluation of trading consistency is to look at winning runs and losing runs in the same way. Winning and losing runs should be distributed as evenly as possible throughout the test period. The smaller the standard deviation, the more consistent and predictable the outcome of the trading model.

The more robust and confidence-building model is one that features:

- The most even distribution of profit and loss.
- The most even distribution of wins and losses.
- The most even distribution of winning and losing runs.

THE MAXIMUM DRAWDOWN

Because maximum drawdown plays such a definitive role in the assessment of the trading model from the viewpoint of risk, it entails a few extra considerations.

Maximum drawdown must be judged in terms of the other losing runs generated by the trading model. By definition, it is the biggest losing run, but how much bigger is an important question. It is a sign of a robust model that the maximum drawdown is, for example, only 20% to 40% larger than the average losing run.

Conversely, you would not want the maximum drawdown to be 300% of the average losing run, unless it were caused by a price shock. A *price shock* is an unusually large price change. By definition, price shocks are outliers or statistical anomalies that occur infrequently. The crash of 1987 was just such a price shock. Price shocks are often caused by significant business, economic, or political events such as the outbreak of war, the unexpected collapse of a major company, a major oil find, or the assassination of a major political leader. Their impact can lead to a windfall or an unusually large loss. They cannot be predicted, only defended against.

It is helpful to examine the market conditions in which the maximum drawdown occurs. Generally speaking, drawdowns occur either in congested markets, or in highly volatile, choppy markets. Both conditions are quite antithetical to optimum trading performance. Therefore, it is a positive sign if the maximum drawdown of the trading model occurred during a period featuring such adverse conditions.

It would be quite troublesome if the maximum drawdown occurred as a long run of losses during market conditions that are indistinguishable from those that produced the largest winning sequence. Trading models usually prosper during strong and sustained trends or periods of high volatility accompanied by strong, clean price swings. Maximum drawdown during such a period should call into question the validity of the trading model.

THE BIGGEST WINNING RUN

The biggest winning run should be evaluated in a manner similar to the biggest losing run. Optimal trading conditions for the trading model are identified by the market conditions that prevailed when the biggest winning run occurred. As noted, most trading systems excel in periods of strong trends, high volatility, and clean price swings. If the maximum winning run occurred during such a market condition, it is consistent with theoretical expectations. If, however, it occurred in markedly different conditions, this should be noted.

The biggest winning run should be compared with the average winning run. For consistency, the closer it is to the average winning run, the more consistent the model. In addition, the biggest winning run should not account for a disproportionate amount of total profit.

9

THE MANY FACES OF OVERFITTING

WHAT IS OVERFITTING?

Overfitting is optimization done wrong. More technically, overfitting or overoptimizing a trading model means finding parameters that closely conform to the price data but have no forecasting ability.

Overfitting is easy to recognize. It occurs when the rules of testing and optimization have been broken. Overfitting is readily detected by its effects: The trading model will perform differently in real-time trading than it did in optimization.

To understand overfitting correctly in an intuitive sense requires some explanation. To understand *overfit*, the word *fit* in the context of trading model development must first be defined and understood.

One definition of the word *fit* in *Webster's II* is: *To be suitable or appropriate to.*

According to this definition, to fit a trading model to price data would be to make it suitable or appropriate for the purpose of trading. To make a trading model requiring model parameters that need to be adapted to price data suitable for trading calls for an effective method of defining these parameters from the price data.

To fit a trading model to price data for the purpose of real-time trading profit, the price data must be analyzed so as to provide model parameters suitable for this purpose. A properly fit, or correctly optimized trading model will perform essentially the same in real-time trading as it did during the optimization or fitting process. In other words, a trading model fit to price data that shows a profit during this process will show a similar profit when used in real-time trading.

Another definition of the word *fit* in *Webster's II* is: *To be the proper size and shape for.*

The parameters of a trading model that fit the price data on which it has been tested are of a "proper size and shape" to generate profit in real-time trading.

The definition of the prefix *over* in *Webster's II* is "excessively." An overfit trading model, therefore, is a trading model that is "excessively fit." Extending this notion of excessively fit to the first definition of *fit,* an overfit trading model is *not suitable or appropriate* for the purpose of real-time trading. Adapting this idea to the second definition of *fit,* the parameters of an overfit trading model exceed the proper size and shape required to produce trading profit.

An overfit trading model has parameters that exceed the correct fit of the price data. From a slightly different view, an overfit trading model has inappropriate parameters for the purpose of real-time trading profit.

The primary technical distinction of an overfit trading model from a properly tested one is a very large difference between the optimization and real-time performance profiles. The practical implication of this difference is usually seen as great profits during optimization with no correlation (often excessive losses) during real-time trading.

To emphasize the point, *overfitting* occurs when the line between correct and incorrect trading model optimization is crossed. This line is easy to cross, which is why it is essential to follow rigorously all the correct testing and optimization procedures. This chapter will clarify the distinction between overfitting and optimization.

Although many different terms have been used to talk about this subject, we view the terms "curve fitting," "overfitting," "overoptimization," and "incorrect optimization" as synonymous. Because of misunderstanding the nature of optimization, some people have incorrectly equated optimization with overfitting. As a consequence of this error, optimization in some circles has unfairly earned a bad reputation.

We use the term *overfitting* to refer to an incorrectly executed optimization that isolates trading model parameters *incapable* of producing real-time trading profits.

We use the term *optimization* to refer to a correct test procedure that isolates the *appropriate* or most reasonable trading model parameters for producing real-time trading profits.

The Case of the Overfit Forecasting Model

Consider a statistician who is building a forecasting model of the stock market. One of the most common and effective ways to do this would be to build a model using regression analysis. In this method, the statistician fits a straight line to the stock market data. After this has been done, the next point on the line of regression is calculated to obtain a forecast. Such a model will give a straight-line projection. Although the projection might not be very accurate from the point of view of trading, it is a sound statistical procedure.

After evaluating the resultant forecasts of this model, the statistician decides to try to improve its accuracy. By observation, the statistician notes that the stock market had a few large rallies and declines. Looking further for other available statistical methods, he fits a curve to the data that can adjust to the contours of the rally and decline. Inspection of this forecasting model shows that it fits the past data a little better than the first forecasting model.

If a little is good, more is better, so the statistician decides to use an equation that can incorporate a curve for every peak and valley in the price data. This is commonly called a "higher order" equation. The resulting forecasting model fits the historical price data more closely than the previous two models. Seeing this, the statistician is already picking out the mansion he plans to buy and the color Mercedes in which he will commute between it and his trading firm.

The mansion burns and the Mercedes crashes when the statistician starts to trade with this forecasting model. The forecasts that it makes in real time have a much larger error term than those calculated during testing. It proves to be much less accurate than the first forecasting model.

What went wrong? The attempt to build a statistically sound forecasting model turned into an exercise in overfitting. Why? Because the statistician abandoned sound statistical theory in the construction of his forecasting model. Instead, he was seduced by the powerful illusion of a mathematical curve with an extraordinary fit to past data. This scenario turned into a classic case of overfitting.

The forecasting model was judged solely on the closeness of its fit to past price data. As a consequence, the statistician consumed too many degrees of freedom with too many constraints and cramped the variable space, resulting in a poor model. To make matters worse, the statistician did no out-of-sample or walk-forward testing of the forecasting model to determine its forecasting abilities with unfamiliar data.

The first forecasting model had a rough fit to the price data. The forecasts from the first model had broad confidence bands that proved to be untradable. But the model had statistical validity. It was developed with sufficient degrees of freedom, that is, a correct number of constraints, or variables, with reference to the sample size. The forecasting model was verified with out-of-sample testing.

The last forecasting model had a close fit to the price data. However, the forecasts from this model proved to be completely inaccurate. This model had no statistical validity because it was developed with insufficient degrees of freedom and too many constraints (i.e., rules or variables). The forecasting model was never verified with out-of-sample testing.

The statistician paid attention only to how "beautifully" the model fit the price data. This attitude stemmed from the false belief that the closeness of fit of the forecasting model to past data is a measure of the predictive value of the model. Proper statistical modeling procedures must always be followed when building a forecasting model, just as proper optimization procedures must be followed when building a trading model.

There is a saying among time series modelers: "Given enough variables, a curve can be perfectly fit to any time series." However, will this beautifully fit curve have any predictive value? Probably not, if attention was not paid to the rules of model construction. Too many constraints and too little data make for a bad model.

This is not to say that a model that fits the underlying data well is necessarily bad. It all comes down to the fact that any type of model can only predict that portion of the data caused by nonrandom movement. A model operating within its natural capabilities is properly fit when its parameters are adapted to the *nonrandom* portion of price movement. A model is improperly fit or overfit when its parameters are adapted to the *random* portion of price movement.

As a footnote, remember that the whole issue of random and nonrandom price movement is a very complicated, technical, and controversial area. The magnitude of random relative to nonrandom price action presents a natural limit to the effectiveness of models. The inability of a forecasting or trading model accurately to predict or trade a market can also be caused by the natural limits inherent in the rules of the model. The "resolution" of the tools might be too "rough" to measure and predict certain types of price action with any degree of accuracy.

The Case of the Overfit Trading Model

The same errors of procedure that gave rise to the overfit statistical model will also give rise to an overfit trading system. Given enough variables and enough scanning, many trading systems can look profitable during optimization. However, simply because a trading system looks profitable during optimization is no guarantee that it will generate real-time trading profits.

Consider an analogous example of a trader optimizing a single moving average trading system. The moving average is scanned over a range of values from 3 to 15 days in steps of 1 day on two years of price data. As a result of this optimization, the trader finds that one set of parameters for this model has made $10,000 in two years with a $5,000 drawdown. It is forward tested for a six-month period. In this period, it made $2,000. These are good results. It worked in forward trading at a pace roughly comparable to its annual rate of $5,000 per year during optimization. So far, so good.

However, the now overeager trader unwittingly abandons caution. A second moving average is added as a measure of a longer trend and is scanned from 10 to 100 days in steps of 5 days. The first moving average is scanned from 1 to 31 days in steps of 2 days. The trader now finds a place where the optimization profit has jumped to $25,000 for the two-year period with a drawdown of still only $5,000. The trader becomes even more frenzied in light of this fantastic increase in performance. In his excitement, he skips the out-of-sample test of this optimization.

Reasoning that the addition of a second variable boosted performance by over 150%, the trader adds two more variables to the model. He now scans the moving averages in the same way as he did in the second test. A buy volatility band is scanned from 0% to 5% in steps of .25% and a sell volatility band over the same range. At the end of this optimization, profit has soared to $65,000 for the two-year period, with a drawdown of only $7,500.

At this point, the trader is simply beside himself. He can't wait until Monday (fortunately, it is Saturday) to start making money. Frustrated, he "settles for" an out-of-sample test. Much to his surprise, the trading system loses $15,000 in a six-month out-of-sample test. Yet, the last optimization was more than 600% better than the first. What went wrong? The same thing that went wrong with the forecaster. The trader paid no attention to degrees of freedom, variable scan lengths, data sample size, and out-of-sample, forward testing. Fortunately, he did one forward test, and the truth was out before the system was traded in real time, where the losses would have been more than a blow to his ego.

A trading model that has been correctly tested, optimized, and walk-forward tested should perform in real time in a way similar to the way it performed during optimization. Correct testing procedures are strictly attentive to all the necessary considerations: (1) sufficient data, (2) sufficient number of markets, (3) degrees of freedom, (4) all the optimization rules, (5) distribution of trades and profits, and (6) walk-forward verification. The trading model developer who pays strict attention to all these guidelines has done all that can be done. The rest is up to the markets.

The Symptoms of an Overfit Trading Model

Nothing could be simpler than describing the real-time symptoms of an overfit trading model: real-time losses. Obviously, all trading systems have losses; but they also have wins. In other words, the minute the model begins to trade in real time, it shows that it has no predictive value and cannot interact with real price action in any way productive of real-time profit. Its real-time trading performance is completely different from actions based on testing.

In more subtle cases, the performance in real time might differ from the testing profile in varying degrees. For example, the average loss string of the test profile might be 3 losses in a row with a dollar value of $4,000. The average win string might be 2 in a row with a dollar value of $6,500. In real time, the average loss string might prove to be $6,000 and four in a row and the average win string might be $4,000 and two in a row. This is obviously no disaster; yet it may be a symptom that all is not well.

It is perfectly possible that an overfit trading model can, by chance, deliver a profit or two or three after which it sinks into the oblivion of unending losses. Such a situation is even worse than the first case because the unsophisticated trader is more confused by such a turn of events. The random profits can delude the trader into thinking that there is just something a "little bit" wrong with this model. It may be true, but it is most likely false.

Another subtle symptom of overfitting can only be detected by comparing the walk-forward efficiency of the trading model with its real-time performance. Recall that walk-forward efficiency is the ratio of average annualized walk-forward profit and average annualized optimization profit. Real-time efficiency should be relatively close to walk-forward efficiency. If it is radically different over a reasonable period of time, it is likely to be a symptom of overfitting. However, this type of situation is usually repairable. If the model passed a walk-forward test, it is probably a sound model. If it is underperforming in real-time based on its test profile, the sound model may have been slightly overoptimized. For example, perhaps the data sample is a bit too small, degrees of freedom are on the edge of insufficient, or the variable scan ranges are a bit too fine. Such errors can be corrected and the original testing procedure can be modified and redone.

THE CAUSES OF OVERFITTING

Violation of the rules of testing and optimization is the cause of overfitting. These violations are of six types:

1. Too many rules and conditions, limiting degrees of freedom.
2. Data sample too small.
3. Incomplete analysis of trading performance.
4. Incomplete analysis of optimization results.
5. Incorrect optimization methods.
6. Lack of postoptimization verification.

Degrees of Freedom

It is a cardinal rule of statistical modeling that too many constraints will lead to incorrect results. In other words, if the variables of a trading model use up too much of the price data, or if there are very few trades relative to the number of rules and amount of data, then the optimization results are questionable. Degrees of freedom are inextricably intertwined with questions of sample size. Placing too many restrictions on the price data is a primary cause of overfitting.

To a large extent, degrees of freedom applied to testing is an attempt to quantify the relationship of sample size with respect to condition. There are two ways to consider degrees of freedom.

Degrees of Freedom Based on Data Size

In order to use degrees of freedom with data, consider each data point that is needed in any type of calculation to represent one degree of freedom. Each rule in a trading model uses, at minimum, one degree of freedom.

Consider two examples using a data sample with a four data-point, two-year, price history that comprises opens, highs, lows, and closes, or, a total of 2,080 data points.

The first system uses a 10-day average of highs and a 50-day average of lows. Average one uses 11 degrees of freedom: 10 highs plus 1 more as a rule. Average two uses 51 degrees of freedom: 50 lows plus 1 as a rule. The total is 62 degrees of freedom used.

The second system uses a 10-day average of closes and a 50-day average of closes. Average one uses 11 degrees of freedom: 10 closes plus 1 as a rule. Average two uses only 41 degrees of freedom: 40 additional closes plus 1 as a rule. The total is 52 degrees of freedom used. Note that data points used twice are counted once.

Degrees of Freedom and Confidence

It is inherent in the precept of statistical modeling that too many rules and constraints will lead to unreliable results. In other words, if there are too many variables in a trading model (with respect to the amount of trades selected, or even the amount of data) then the optimization results are questionable. This was briefly discussed in Chapter 4.

Placing too many restrictions on the price data is the primary cause of overfitting. But it is not always clear to the developer that he or she is guilty of this action. For example, on each new day the system has a choice of selecting one of 250 rules to apply. A rule can be very specific, such as, "Buy and hold for a $250 profit." Using the hindside allowed by iterative computer testing, the correct selection can be found for profiting from each day's move during the past year. Then we have the following relationship

$$f(250 \text{ days}, 250 \text{ rules}) = \text{Perfect trading}$$

But that was obvious to everyone. Using just two rules (buy and sell) applied specifically to each day will also produce a large profit—but not as large as case (1). This looks as follows

$$f(250 \text{ days}, 2 \text{ rules}) = \text{Profits daily}$$

Because the rules aren't specific enough to capture profits at their daily maximum, we'll have to settle for suboptimal hypothetical profits. But this is another case of knowing which rule to apply by looking ahead at the data to see which worked. That's not the choice in real trading.

Practical optimization often involves a more subtle form of overfitting. This may be

- Adding rules one at a time to watch how performance improves (and discarding those that don't work), and

- Testing many variations of the same rule (i.e., the speed of a moving average).

It is inevitable that the search for profits involves observing the previous test run (or set of tests), finding the objectionable trades and formulating new rules to correct the event. Sometimes these rules improve results; often they cause equally difficult problems in another time period.

Each new rule tested, whether used or rejected, is one of those degrees of freedom gone, never to be recovered. If you find one rule that worked by testing 250, have you found the true market pattern?

Consider this: You found that coffee production in Brazil exactly forecasts the subsequent (2 months later) grain harvest in North Africa in all of the past 20 years. This is important because it allows the demand for grain to be identified. Further study shows that this relationship can be explained because of the Gulf Stream, which flows from the eastern coast of South America to the Mideast, affecting the climate. Would you take advantage of this relationship. Perhaps.

What if you were told that, to find this 20 of 20 success, 100 different countries were matched, and only one was successful? What if that relationship had failed for the 5-years prior to the period demonstrated? What you don't know can hurt. Similarly, testing many rules and conditions, shortening the data period, and narrowing the range of the variables are all subtle ways of deceiving yourself.

Degrees of freedom is a way of keeping count of this transgression. Look at two extremes. First, you define a system by the rules: *buy when today's close is greater than the past 3 closes and today's low is greater than yesterday's low,* and *close-out the position when today's open or low is below yesterday's low.*

Perhaps this reflects some observation that you have made during the past few years of watching the market. You run this through 5 years of daily data and it is profitable 4 of 5 years, returning 30% per year. It confirms your theory. You have used 2 rules and one test on 1,250 days of data, producing 350 trades. That satisfies all criteria.

Another trader believes that a moving average system will work, as long as the risk is controlled. He tests 1,250 days of data for 49 moving averages ranging from 2 to 50, and for 20 stop losses from $50 to $1,000 in increments of $50, or 980 combinations. The results show that 20% of these tests are profitable, and the best gives a 70% return. But 980 tests were performed on 1,250 data points. That must severely reduce your confidence in the results and leave the question "Is it the correct system, or another Gulf Stream justification?"

The first case is clearly ideal. Justifying a theory on the first try is a lot to ask for. But the principle is important. Think carefully before you add and test another rule. Make each one your last, because every one reduces the degrees of freedom, and therefore your confidence. Think of it as taking a picture with film that cost $100,000 per frame.

To ensure statistical validity, at least 90% degrees of freedom must remain after all rules, indicators, and start-up overhead are deducted. Degrees of freedom can be overconstrained by:

1. A data sample that is too small.
2. Too much start-up overhead.
3. Too many rules.
4. Too many variables (any model element that uses data).

Most trading software, unfortunately, does not calculate degrees of freedom. They must be known and are a very important element in the design of the testing process. Too few degrees of freedom is one of the most common causes of overfitting.

Fortunately, common sense, along with careful crafting of the design and setup of the testing and optimization process can easily remedy this omission. Use a large enough test sample. Allow for start-up overhead. Test with degrees of freedom better than 90% whenever possible. In the case of degrees of freedom, more is definitely better.

Sample Size

The size of the test sample has a large impact on another area essential to proper testing. The sample size must be large enough to allow the trading system to generate a statistically significant sample of trades. A sample of one trade is certainly insignificant, whereas a sample of 50 trades or more is generally adequate. However, constraints imposed by a trading system or restrictions on data availability may occasionally force a judgment on a trade sample that is less than 30. If this is the case, the analyst must be even more cautious in every other category.

The formula for standard error is a helpful guide here. The following four examples show a sample that is too small, a sample of 50, one of 100, and one of 300:

$$\text{Standard Error} = 1/\sqrt{\text{Sample Size}}$$

Sample of 10 trades
$$\text{Standard Error} = 1/\sqrt{10}$$
$$= 1/3.162$$
$$= 31.6\%$$

Sample of 50 trades
$$\text{Standard Error} = 1/\sqrt{50}$$
$$= 1/7.07$$
$$= 14.1\%$$

Sample of 100 trades
$$\text{Standard Error} = 1/\sqrt{100}$$
$$= 1/10$$
$$= 10\%$$

Sample of 300 trades
$$\text{Standard Error} = 1/\sqrt{300}$$
$$= 1/17.3$$
$$= 5.7\%$$

Trading pace will vary from system to system. For example, a long-term trading system that trades, for example, 2 to 4 times a year, will require more data to achieve 50 trades. In addition, it will have indicators that use many degrees of freedom and will add a larger start-up overhead. Conversely, a short-term system that trades twice a week will need less data to achieve 50 trades, will use far fewer degrees of freedom, and will have a lighter start-up overhead.

The Evaluation of Trades

Whereas the incorrect evaluation of trades is not strictly a cause of overfitting, it is sufficiently abused to be a common cause of failure. It is therefore worth emphasizing through repetition. As detailed in Chapter 8, an inaccurate evaluation of the trade sample can lead to the real-time failure of a model.

One trade should not account for more than 30% of total profit, especially if the trade sample is more than two or three years in size. Winning trades must be evenly distributed throughout the sample, the more evenly the better. This points to a more consistent trading model.

Losing trades also must be evenly distributed throughout. Again, the more evenly, the better.

The distribution of profit and loss should be even from period to period, for example, from month to month, or quarter to quarter. The more evenly distributed, the better. Any excessive concentrations are suspect. The more evenly distributed, the more consistent and, therefore, the more reliable the trading model.

The Evaluation of the Optimization

The incorrect interpretation of optimization results can lead to overfitting. Recalling that optimization is a tool for finding a robust trading strategy, the results of a sequence of optimization tests should prove the soundness of the method. This would be the case if a large percentage of tests were profitable, regardless of the specific parameters (i.e., the length of the moving average or the size of the stop-loss) used in those tests.

First, the tests must include a broad range of parameters that are considered feasible inputs. This may be moving average speeds from 2 days to 100 days, and maximum losses of $50 to $5,000. The distribution of tests should be such that the number of trades changes evenly across the different moving average speeds. This means testing wider intervals as the moving average days get larger.

A robust test result is one in which the average of all tests is positive. Better still, the average of all tests is positive by 1 standard deviation. That is equivalent to 67% of all tests being profitable.

Results with lower returns would be acceptable if the profitable tests were all grouped and continued to show stable, positive results as parameters increased or decreased to the extremes tested. For example, moving averages from 2 to 20 days were not profitable, but improved as the number of days increased. Profits appeared when the tested interval moved over 20 days, peaking at 35 days, and remained profitable from 35 to 100 days.

Erratic results—those which have no apparent pattern—must be rejected. Isolated areas of success, no matter how profitable, represent a special combination of parameters that work on a particular market pattern and does not indicate a robust strategy; instead, it should be considered "fine tuning."

Changes to rules and modification of the trading strategy should improve the average of all tests without increasing the standard deviation. This shows a global improvement, rather than fitting specific price patterns.

Profit Spikes

Another common cause of overfitting is the selection of a profit spike as a top model. Recall that a *profit spike* is a profitable model with either much less profitable or losing models for neighbors. (See Figure 7–2.) This is a difficult problem because most commercial trading software will accept a profit spike as an acceptable model. Some evaluation methods tend to minimize this problem. Looking at more than one top model is a way to overcome this problem. Looking at an average of the top model and its neighbors is another solution to this problem.

A profit spike is a poor choice. It is a statistical anomaly produced by a set of trading parameters with near calamitous falloff on models that are only one step away. For example, assume a moving average model produces a $20,000 profit with a 10-day average. The 9-day average shows a profit of $3,000 and the 11-day average has a loss of ($2,000). This is disastrous. The 10-day model performs poorly one step each way. This 10-day average trading model is an unacceptable profit spike and is probably a statistical outlier.

In contrast, consider the same model with a $20,000 profit at the 10-day average. The 9-day average shows a profit of $18,000 and the 11-day average has a profit of $19,000. This is a more robust trading model.

A profit spike is not the best choice for trading purposes. Evaluating a top model in light of its neighbors is a better way to isolate a robust trading model.

Overscanning

Another direct cause of overfitting is an improper optimization method called *overscanning*, which occurs in two ways. The first is performing a scan of a variable using a step size that is initially too small and inconsistent across the optimization. The second occurs when a profitable range of variables is isolated and then scanned again with smaller steps.

To illustrate how the first type of abuse occurs, consider a two moving-average system. The first average tracks changes in the short-term trend. Such trends will vary in length from 2 to 10 days. A 3-day trend is very different from a 4-day trend since it uses 1/3 more data. It is therefore reasonable to optimize this average from 2 to 10 days at steps of 1 day.

The second average test changes in the long-term trend. Such trends might vary in length from 30 to 100 days. Because this average measures long-term trends, the results of a 90-day average are very similar to those of a 91-day average that varies only 1/90 in the amount of data used. Therefore, optimizing this average from 30 to 100 days in steps of 1 would be considered too fine; it is inconsistent with the step size in the first moving average.

Looking again at the theory behind the trading system, it is clear that a change from a 90- to a 95-day average represents a change consistent with the rest of the test space. Therefore, optimizing this average from 30 to 100 days in steps of 5 is appropriate.

The consequences of overscanning by using a constant or incorrect step size is that the test results do not give a fair survey of the strategy. In the most common case the longer trend speeds appear in a larger percentage of the tests while some of the faster trading models may be missed entirely.

Narrowing the Scan Range

It is inevitable that, once a profitable subset of the original scan ranges has been isolated, a series of finer scans will be performed. The intention is to zero in on the most profitable combination of parameters. Although there is value in this procedure, it may introduce error.

Narrowing the scan range to a known profitable area will, by definition, raise the average performance of the entire series of new tests. What does this accomplish? Used properly, it can show

- Consistency over the tested ranges,

- Inconsistency indicating overfitting or unstable results, and

- The distribution of performance which allows better parameter selection.

Once this restricted test has been done, and the results analyzed, there will be a tendency to make changes to the strategy that correct problems or increase profits. Rerunning tests on this same narrow scan range will prove the success of those changes in a specific market pattern. But are these changes robust? This can only be known by rerunning the original, broad scan range to see if the average of all test results were improved. Changes that improve only a small group of tests are fine-tuning, or overfitting the data. This technique appears to produce improved results but has no forecasting ability. Narrowing the scan range is a valuable method of looking for problems, but should not be used to test new rules and conditions.

THE WALK-FORWARD TEST

The role of the walk-forward test in combating overfitting looms large. All necessary cautions must, as a matter of good form, be used each and every time testing or optimization is done. However, the walk-forward analysis is an essential part of testing. No matter how well a trading system performs in testing and optimization, if it does not "walk forward" (i.e., perform as well on out-of-sample, postoptimization trading), the trading model does not work. This is discussed in Chapter 7.

It is worth repeating that a bad model can look great with the benefit of overfitting. Conversely, excessive optimization can make a good model look bad in a walk-forward analysis. The calculation of the walk-forward efficiency is one of the benefits of the walk-forward analysis.

How does the walk-forward analysis uncover optimization excesses? The most important measure is whether or not it made a profit in the walk forward. The secondary measure is the pace or degree of efficiency at which it made a walk-forward profit. The first is obvious and needs no more discussion.

The question of walk-forward efficiency is little known and more subtle. As stated in Chapter 7, a properly optimized model will make walk-forward profits in a manner that is generally consistent with the way it traded during optimization. In other words, assume a trading model generates the following optimization profile:

- Profits of $10,000 a year.
- 12 trades per year.
- 65% wins and 35% losses.
- Drawdown of $4,000 in 4 trades.
- Average winning run of 2 trades for $2,500.
- Average losing run of 3 trades for $1,500.

Remember that this optimization profile is an average of many different optimizations. If the model is properly optimized and market conditions remain within the bounds of those included in the optimization data, then postoptimization or walk-forward performance should be quite similar to the profile over a reasonable period of time.

Recall that the walk-forward efficiency (WFE) statistic produced during a walk-forward test is a ratio of average annual walk-forward profit and average annual optimization profit. The formula is

WFE   : Walk-Forward Efficiency
AAOP   : Average Annualized Optimization Profit
AAWFP : Average Annualized Walk-Forward Profit
WFE   = AAWP/AAOP

This measure makes evaluation very easy. It is good if a walk-forward test produces a profit and a WFE of at least 50%. The closer the WFE is to 100%, the better. It has been observed that a properly optimized trading model can produce walk-forward and real-time profits that exceed the pace of optimization for a short period. This can occur for a trend-following moving-average system when a market goes into a strong trend accompanied by good swing volatility and increased liquidity. In other words, a trading model can outperform its optimization profile when it starts trading in a very accommodating market.

Consider a situation that differs from the ideal one described previously in which a trading model is performing exceptionally well in optimization. The model is making a modest profit in the walk forward with a very low WFE of 10%. What does this mean? The model is working because it shows a postoptimization profit. However, it is at a very low level of efficiency.

This can be the result of three things. The model might simply be poor: sound but not terribly efficient for whatever reason. If this is the case, the model should be rejected or design modifications should be considered. Second, the model might be overoptimized, with insufficient attention to degrees of freedom, sample size, number of variables, scan ranges, and so on. If this is determined to be the cause, the solution is another walk-forward test that is properly designed. The third, and more subtle cause, is that the walk-forward test window size may be too small and, as a result, the model is cramped and cannot perform as it should. An experiment with different estimation and test window sizes may be the solution.

Summary

The walk-forward analysis must be the final arbiter of the reality of a trading model. If a trading model passes the walk-forward test with profit, consistency, and a respectable WFE, it is a model that can be traded in real time with confidence. If a trading model shows losses in the walk-forward test, it is the end of the road. If a trading model shows a nominal profit and low WFE, it needs more work.

10

THE EVALUATION OF
REAL-TIME TRADING

The path from trading idea to implementation, through refinement, testing, and optimization, is a long one. It is well worth it, however, when the well-conceived and thoroughly tested trading model starts to produce real-time profits.

Before the age of the microcomputer, it was all too common to begin trading a good idea after what would now be viewed as cursory and inadequate testing. The outcome was usually losing trades. The reason is clear to all readers who have come this far in this book.

The advent of the microcomputer is a money saver in many ways. However, the microcomputer primarily saves the trader money by keeping bad trades out of the trading account. Computer time, no matter how much is used, is usually a lot cheaper than untested and therefore avoidable trading losses.

After a trading model has passed through thorough testing with robust profit, it must still be continuously evaluated in real-time trading. There are three ways of judging real-time performance:

1. Return on investment.
2. Maximum loss.
3. Real-time compared with test performance.

RETURN ON INVESTMENT

Just as the profit performance of a trading model during testing must be compared with other investments that compete for the trading dollar, so must real-time performance. Although this may seem obvious, comparative return on investment is one of the three critical measures of real-time performance.

If the return on investment of the trading model pales in comparison with other investments, the trader as a prudent businessperson must make a decision. It must be determined why performance is low compared with other investments. This can be caused by four factors:

1. A poor trading strategy.
2. A contraction of market opportunity.
3. The emergence of a new, superior investment or trading model.
4. The failure of the model to hold up in real time compared with test performance.

Poor Strategy

If, for any reason, a trading model is performing at a level below financial expectation, the only alternative is to abandon it in favor of superior vehicles that are outshining it. Of course, the trader can always return to the drawing board in an effort to enhance the strategy.

Market Contraction

A contraction in market activity is generally a time when a market offers little profit opportunity. Such a contraction is usually characterized by low volatility and a nontrending market. Prices can spend days, weeks, months, or even years in such a low-opportunity condition.

A knowledge of the historical characteristics of the market can help in the formation of an informed business decision. For example, consider a market that is prone to extended periods of low volatility sideways price action. If the market has been in such a period for the last few months, this may be reason to abandon the trading model in favor of other superior opportunities in more active markets, even though it is performing according to expectation.

If the trader discovers a superior investment or trading model, he must objectively evaluate both investments on a feature-by-feature basis and pick the superior one. To be superior, the trading vehicle would need a better return on investment at the same risk or the same return at a lower risk.

There is a more complicated decision process to follow if the trading model is performing at a level below expectation compared with trading performance during testing. This is covered in detail in the section "Real-time Compared with Test Performance."

MAXIMUM LOSS

The second major consideration in the evaluation of real-time performance is the risk of losing too much trading capital to sustain trading. Prior to trading, a loss threshold or system stop-loss must be established that dictates when to abandon a trading model.

The factors that determine this level are:

1. The minimum trading capital necessary for continued financing of the margin required to trade at the same commitment.
2. A decision to limit losses to a predetermined percentage of trading capital.
3. A drawdown exceeding a predetermined percentage of the maximum drawdown that occurred during testing.

All three criteria are based on considerations of where current performance would have failed to represent expectations.

This loss threshold or limit is known as the *system stop-loss*. Trading of the system ceases if it generates losses that exceed the system stop-loss. For example, if the system stop-loss is determined to be $10,000 based on an investment of $30,000, then trading is stopped when losses exceed this amount.

The system stop-loss is based on the cost of trading and the risk profile of the model defined during testing. A system stop-loss is calculated as follows:

Maximum Drawdown	:	$5,000
Drawdown Safety Factor	:	2
System Stop-Loss	:	Maximum Drawdown × Safety Factor
System Stop-Loss	:	$5,000 × 2
System Stop-Loss	:	$10,000

The trading system stop-loss is analogous to the stop-loss order placed on an open position. Just as a stop-loss order limits the amount of capital that will be risked per trade, the system stop-loss limits how much trading capital will be risked on the trading system as a whole. Consequently, it should be viewed in the same light and applied with the same consistency. The need for the system stop-loss is the reason it is necessary to measure the risk of a trading system accurately.

A sound trading system will generate losing runs. Trading can continue only as long as there is sufficient trading capital. A properly calculated system stop-loss will determine the amount of trading capital necessary to continue trading after a natural losing run has occurred. Conversely, trading will cease if a losing run occurs in excess of expectation.

The test profile will identify the dollar amount of the maximum drawdown. To allow for changes in volatility and sample error, the actual system stop-loss should be a multiple of this number. Changes in volatility should be considered in setting this loss limit. In other words, if it is known that the maximum drawdown is $4,000 based on an average daily volatility of 4 points, then a maximum drawdown of $6,000 is appropriate for an average daily volatility of 6 points.

The safety factor, that is, a predetermined value by which the maximum drawdown is multiplied, is based on the conservative assumption that test results can be exceeded. For example, with a safety factor of 2, a $4,000 maximum drawdown will be doubled to produce a system stop-loss of $8,000.

Maximum drawdown can be exceeded, for example, if a period of congestion occurs that is longer than any encountered during testing. It can also be exceeded if volatility is greater than that of the price action that produced the maximum drawdown.

In fact, many professional traders calculate a system stop-loss at 3 times the maximum drawdown. For example, if the maximum drawdown is $5,000, then a system stop-loss equal to $300% of this, or $15,000, will be set at the start of trading. Required capital will be margin plus this system stop-loss so that even if losses 3 times maximum drawdown occur, the system can still be traded.

Preservation of Capital

The system stop-loss is also dictated by the preservation of capital. No matter how profitable the trading system, it is highly unlikely to lead to profit if it is traded in an undercapitalized account. All trading systems have a minimum capital requirement. The way to calculate *required capital* is to add together required margin with a multiple of the maximum drawdown. For example, assume a margin of $5,000 per contract, a drawdown of $5,000, and risk multiple of 3. Required capital to trade the system then is $20,000. It is calculated as follows: margin of $5,000 plus 3 times the drawdown of $5,000, which is $20,000.

Another consideration is to set, in advance of trading, a percentage of trading capital that can be lost before trading is stopped. This can be an alternative to the system stop-loss. It is another approach to capital preservation. For example, assume a 40% capital loss limit and a $25,000 account. If losses exceed $10,000 ($25,000 × .4 = $10,000), trading is stopped. It is important to calculate these so as to be consistent with the trading requirements based on an analysis of risk. To harmonize both of these requirements, required trading capital is calculated as follows:

System Stop-Loss = Maximum Drawdown × Safety Factor
System Stop-Loss = $5,000 × 3
System Stop-Loss = $15,000
Required Capital = System Stop-Loss/Capital Stop-Loss
Required Capital = $15,000/40%
Required Capital = $37,500

In this way, the system stop-loss and the capital stop-loss are one and the same; that is, a loss of $15,000, which accommodates the system stop-loss, is also the capital stop-loss ($37,500 × 40% = $15,000).

REAL-TIME COMPARED WITH TEST PERFORMANCE

Most often, a system is judged by its profit. Profit motivates the trader to continue trading. However, a second level of judgment evaluates the "quality" of this profit. Its real-time trading performance must be judged within the context of what is known about the trading model based on the way it performed during testing. A trading model is functioning properly if its real-time trading performance is "equivalent" to its testing performance. In the simplest of terms, if a trading model produced an average monthly profit of $1,000 in testing, then a performance of three months of $2,000 real-time losses is not "equivalent."

Real-time trading can begin just as easily with a profitable or a losing run, or with a winning run. Either type of real-time trading performance can be readily accepted if it is consistent with the profile found during testing. The purpose of this section is to discuss what happens when performance is not consistent with testing.

If real-time trading begins with a few losses, often traders say, "The trading model fell apart," and stop trading. Well, maybe it did and maybe it didn't. It is impossible to know if the trading model "fell apart" unless, prior to the start of real-time trading, "falling apart" is precisely defined. Markets do change, and even a good model can generate losses in excess of those found in testing. Good models have losing trades.

The odds that the first real-time trade will be a win or a loss are the same as the ratio of profitability to losing trades found during testing. Real-time performance will probably be slightly worse. The same is true of the odds that the first string of trades will be wins or losses. Most traders are a lot more capable of accepting wins with composure than losses. Surprise, surprise. Yet, a trader must understand that it is good fortune and frequently lower probability, if the first trade is a win. And considering how a first win can inflate the ego of some traders, this might actually prove to be bad luck in the long run.

Before real-time trading begins, it is essential that the trader have a realistic expectation of trading performance grounded in historical testing. Without this, the trader has no way of assessing real-time trading performance, whether profitable or not.

To make this evaluation, the trader needs a detailed statistical evaluation of both testing and real-time trading performance. The *test profile* consists of a set of statistical measures of trading performance found during testing. The *trading profile* consists of the same measures of real-time trading performance.

The following statistical measures must then be recorded for both historical and real-time trading performance:

1. Annualized profit.
2. Number of trades per year.
3. Percentage of winning trades.
4. Largest win.
5. Average win.
6. Length of time of average win.
7. Largest loss.
8. Average loss.
9. Length of time of average loss.
10. Average winning run.
11. Largest winning run.
12. Average losing run.

13. Largest losing run.
14. Maximum equity drawdown.
15. Maximum equity runup.

The maximum balance drawdown is the dollar value of the largest decrease in equity before a new equity high occurs. The maximum balance runup is the dollar value of the largest increase from either the beginning investment or the lowest point of a loss to an equity high.

A run of trades is defined by the number of trades in the run. The following statistics should be kept about these runs:

- The profit or loss.
- The number of trades.
- How long it lasted in days, hours, etc.

To judge the *"quality"* of real-time trading, the trader periodically compares the trading profile with the test profile.

Comparing the Test and Trade Profiles

How soon can a trading model be judged in real-time trading? In truth, not too quickly. Just as in testing, a statistically significant number of trades must be generated to make a sound judgment. Real-time performance cannot be judged based on one win or one loss, unless one of them is a very large outlier.

A flawed model will often show itself clearly with a series of losses that reaches the system stop-loss immediately. If this occurs, trading stops. This is the capital-preserving function of the system stop-loss.

Since a valid trading model can also generate a losing run in the course of regular performance, how can failure be distinguished from correct performance? The answer is found by comparing the test and trade profiles.

A bad model will perform differently from its test profile. For example, assume a model with a test profile that includes a $4,000 drawdown in 3 trades during average volatility. Assume that the standard deviation of the drawdown is $2,000 and 2 trades. Real-time trading produces 7 losses in row for an $8,000 loss, with market conditions the same as that of the test period. What happened? A bad model somehow slipped through the testing process. This actual string of losses exceeds the maximum drawdown of $4,000 plus the standard deviation of $2,000 and the number of trades of 3 plus the standard deviation of 2. This is different enough from expectation to suspend trading.

Consider the same model with a slightly different start: 3 losses totaling $8,000 with volatility at twice the level of the test profile drawdown. This real-time string of losses is the same length but twice the dollar size of the test profile. Note, however, that volatility is double that of the test drawdown. This may be all right. Why? Because when volatility increases, both wins and losses should increase in proportion.

Understanding the Test Profile

Impatience is one of the most common causes of real-time trading failure. Another common cause is an inadequate understanding of the test profile. Nothing is more exciting than a trading model that starts trading with a couple of big wins, but this can also be emotionally destabilizing. The trader, feeling, incorrectly, that he or she can do no wrong, tends to disregard atypical losses that may follow. This can also lead to false confidence, which can encourage excesses, such as doubling the number of contracts that are traded without proper regard to money management. This, in turn, will cause larger losses. Such behavior unsettles the risk-to-reward relationships uncovered during testing.

An unusually large profit can also indicate an error in the trading system. A profit that exceeds expectation is as much an error as a loss that exceeds expectation. An unusually large profit is often caused by increased volatility. It may typically be followed by an unusually large loss. The trader must be careful to reassess the capital requirements of the system based on this higher volatility.

Conversely, nothing is more disturbing to the trader than starting with a few big losses. It causes the trader to doubt the trading model and may lead to destructive second guessing. When the trader selects which trades to take from the trading model, the trader is no longer trading the system. It can also lead to an unwarranted and premature abandonment of the trading model. The next trade may be a typical win, just as the losses were typical.

In another situation, a month of small losses and small wins, leading to little change in profit or loss, can bore the trader. The boredom may lead the trader to abandon the system prematurely in favor of something else, or to increase the size of the trades. Yet, this month might be quite typical of months that occurred during testing, and the trader is unaware of this because the results were not thoroughly studied. The next month may well hold the type of profit the system has promised but has yet to deliver.

To prevent such false judgments, the trader must develop a thorough understanding of how the model trades. This can be accomplished in a number of ways. The first is through careful study of the performance of the trading system on a month-by-month or quarter-by-quarter basis. The trader must become familiar with the performance of the trading system beginning with the macroscopic level and ending with the microscopic level.

The statistical analysis of trading performance illustrated in the Analysis Report in Figure 10–1 presents one macroscopic view. A graphic view of the trades that produced these results is displayed in Figure 10–2. Figure 10–3 lists these trades in a tabular form. Figures 10–1 to 10–4 are shown at the end of this chapter.

The most thorough method of analysis is to study the performance of the trading model on a day-by-day basis. Review all the daily trades, stops, positions, and equity changes. This microscopic evaluation is the only real way to develop a true intuitive, concrete understanding of the performance of the trading system. Figure 10–4 shows nine Daily Reports from 7/1/91 through 7/12/91. This shows daily open equity for open positions with stops and trades.

A working understanding of the performance of the trading model comes from three points of view: macroscopic, interval by interval, and day by day. Coupled with the test and trade profiles, the trader is properly equipped to trade the model in real time.

PERFORMANCE PATTERNS AND QUIRKS

Consider three different real-time trading outcomes. In the first case, the trading model produces fantastic windfall profits. In the second case, the trading model begins with a losing streak. In the third case, the trading model produces a series of small wins and losses.

A Windfall Profit

In the first case of windfall profit, who would complain? No one. Profit is profit. The trader can ignore all the risk management controls. If enough profit is made, the trader might consider early retirement. But it is best not to let greed get the upper hand in such a fortunate situation. The profit is most likely a windfall event. Trading based on the expectation of similar profits is unlikely to be successful.

For example, reports of fantastic profits were heard of after the 1987 crash. A trading firm in Chicago reportedly made more than a billion dollars on their S&P and T-bond positions in a matter of a few days. The principals were reported to have done two things. They paid large bonuses and gave a paid vacation of one month to all employees. The operation was closed for one month while the principals decided what they were going to do with their new incredible wealth. Good idea or bad? One could reason both ways. In truth, the huge profits that amass from such an event are more a windfall than the result of skill or foresight. A good trader knows the difference. Skill keeps a good trader trading in bad times and produces consistent profits during good times. A good trader knows when he or she has been the beneficiary of a windfall and does not expect to be able consistently to reproduce such levels of profit. The beneficiaries of this windfall recognized it as such and took time out to assess its impact.

A winning streak at the start of real-time trading is more welcome than a losing streak. But it must not be allowed to destabilize the trader. The proper attitude is simple: Take the money, smile, and realize that this is luck. It could just as easily have gone the other way. Win or lose, the trade profile must be compared with the test profile. Was the size of the winning run more or less than 50%, or some other predetermined measure, of the average winning run of the test profile? Was the size of the losing run within the preset boundaries of the test profile losing runs? If yes, performance is acceptable. Has volatility changed? Has the trend changed? It is a common mistake of system traders to overly-scrutinize losses and to gleefully and uncritically accept wins.

A Losing Run

In the second case, when real-time trading begins with a losing streak, a trader may panic, often without justification. Real-time trading can go either way. The trading system will produce losses as well as wins. Therefore, this losing streak must be compared with that of its test profile. If it is within expectation, there is no reason to panic. The system stop-loss should be closely monitored until either it is broken or the losing streak ends. Of course, if the system continues to lose and meets and exceeds the loss limit, then trading must be stopped.

Insignificant Production

In the third case, consider when a trading system produces a series of small wins and losses yielding a small net loss or profit after one month of trading. This type of "slow bleed" can prove almost as trying to the trader as a faster run of losses. Traders are not known for their patience. This trade profile must be compared with the test profile. If such a "slow period" is typical of the test profile, then patience is required. If such a period never occurred in testing, it is a warning that either conditions have changed substantially or the trading system is failing.

SUMMARY

There are three requirements to trade a system successfully in real time:

1. The test profile.
2. The system stop-loss.
3. The trade profile.

The first two must be available at the start of trading the system. The trade profile is the result of actual market activity and must be compiled accordingly.

A comparison of each of the statistical measures in the trade and test profiles must be made at periodic intervals. Statistical measures in the trade profile that are less than 50% or more than 150% of the corresponding test profile measure, regardless of whether they are in the win or loss column, must be explained.

Equity drawdowns must be constantly monitored with respect to the system stop-loss. This system stop-loss limit is a cutoff point on the trading system. The system stop-loss is equal to the margin plus the maximum equity drawdown multiplied by a safety factor.

The start of real-time trading is perhaps the most critical time. The shift from testing to trading is significant; it is a leap from idea to reality, from paper trading to trading with real money, and from reason to emotion. The trader can become excessively and uncritically optimistic if the first trade is a win, especially a big one. This can lead to overtrading. Conversely, the trader can become skeptical and overly anxious if the first trade is a loss, especially a big one. This can lead to a premature exit of the system.

In both cases, emotional reactions must be controlled by a strict and rational adherence to the two rules that govern trading of a mechanical system. Continue to trade the system if it performs in real time according to the expectations generated by the test profile and trading equity remains above the system stop-loss.

```
================================================================
              Advanced Trader V1.09 Analysis Report
----------------------------------------------------------------
Contract Traded : S&P 500 Composite      D 03/92        06/03/91 - 12/31/91
Script Name     : C:\PARDO\RPAT\BLAST\BO00.LOG
Trades Analyzed : All
Dollar Factor  :      500.00 Beg. Balance :  25000.00 Interest   :       0.00
Commission     :       50.00 Slippage     :    100.00 Margin     :   10000.00
Maximum Lots   :           1 Equity Limit :      0.00 Max. Positions:        0

Inside Days Filter        :    No !  Outside Days Filter       :     No !
Extreme Outside Filter    :    No !  Extreme Outside Day Perc  :   1000 !
Period of Daily Range Ave :    10 !  Peak & Valley Level       :      1 !
Net Profit/Loss $   12920.00
Total Profit    $   13545.00  Total Loss $   -625.00  Avg. Trade $  2584.00
----------------------------------------------------------------
               : # Trades :   Maximum   :   Minimum   :   Average
----------------------------------------------------------------
Total ........ :    5    : Win   3/ 60% : Loss   2/ 40% :
Win .......... :    3    :    7990.00   :    2240.00   :    4515.00
Win runs ..... :    2    : 10230.00/ 2  :  3315.00/ 1  :  6772.50/ 1
Loss ......... :    2    :   -360.00    :   -265.00    :   -312.50
Loss runs .... :    2    :  -360.00/ 1  :  -265.00/ 1  :  -312.50/ 1
Win/Loss Ratio.:         :      22.19   :      8.45    :     14.45
----------------------------------------------------------------
Open Equity ......... $  19755.00   Open Equity Drawdown . $  -5990.00
Max. Balance Drawback $   -360.00   Max. Equity Profit ... $  12920.00
Reward / Risk ........    35.89 TO 1 Annual rate of return.     322.33
Profit Index .........    21.67
Pessimistic Margin....    46.58   Adjusted Pess. Margin.     -10.67
Pess. Month Avg.......    -2.50   Pess. Month Variance .       3.12
Monthly Net PL Large .  7990.00/9111 Monthly Net PL Small . -360.00/9108
Monthly Net PL Ave ...  2584.00   Modified Pess. Margin.       5.60
================================================================
```

Figure 10-1   Analysis Report

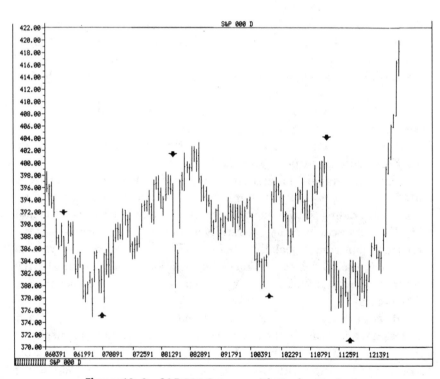

Figure 10-2   S&P 500 Futures with Trades Marked

• 158 •

```
===============================================================================
                        Advanced Trader V1.09 Analysis Report
-------------------------------------------------------------------------------
Contract Traded : S&P 500 Composite    D 03/92        06/03/91 - 12/31/91
Script Name     : C:\PARDO\RPAT\BLAST\BDOO.LOG
Trades Analyzed : All

Trade Order !  Type  !  Entry  !  Price  !! Trade Order ! Type !  Exit   !  Price  !  Net P&L
-------------------------------------------------------------------------------------------------
  O# 2    ! 1 Sell ! 06/12/91 !  382.62 !! O# 1   ! Buy  ! 07/05/91 !  382.85 ! [$   265.00]
  O# 1    ! 1 Buy  ! 07/05/91 !  382.85 !! O# 2   ! Sell ! 08/16/91 !  389.78 ! $  3315.00
  O# 2    ! 1 Sell ! 08/16/91 !  389.78 !! O# 1   ! Buy  ! 10/14/91 !  390.20 ! [$   360.00]
  O# 1    ! 1 Buy  ! 10/14/91 !  390.20 !! O# 2   ! Sell ! 11/15/91 !  394.97 ! $  2240.00
  O# 2    ! 1 Sell ! 11/15/91 !  394.97 !! O# 1   ! Buy  ! 12/02/91 !  378.69 ! $  7990.00
                                                            Net Profit/Loss ! $ 12920.00
  O# 1    ! 1 Buy  ! 12/02/91 !  378.69 !!       open position             ! $ 19755.00
-------------------------------------------------------------------------------------------------
```

Figure 10-3   Trade List

```
=================================================================================
S&P 500 Composite      D 03/92                          Mon.  07/01/91
---------------------------------------------------------------------------------
Open :     382.35  High :     385.35  Low :     380.35  Close :     385.10
---------------------------------------------------------------------------------
Close Status and Tomorrow's Orders
--------------------------------------
Current Positions : SHORT  1 at     382.62 on 06/12/91   (O# 2)

Close Status :  1 SHORT position            Open Equity :   -1240.00

Before the open, place the following orders :
  O# 1              : BUY   2  at     390.18  STOP

=================================================================================
S&P 500 Composite      D 03/92                          Tues.  07/02/91
---------------------------------------------------------------------------------
Open :     384.70  High :     385.50  Low :     384.20  Close :     385.25
---------------------------------------------------------------------------------
Close Status and Tomorrow's Orders
--------------------------------------
Current Positions : SHORT  1 at     382.62 on 06/12/91   (O# 2)

Close Status :  1 SHORT position            Open Equity :   -1315.00

Before the open, place the following orders :
  O# 1              : BUY   2  at     387.75  STOP

=================================================================================
S&P 500 Composite      D 03/92                          Wed.  07/03/91
---------------------------------------------------------------------------------
Open :     382.50  High :     382.50  Low :     378.60  Close :     380.60
---------------------------------------------------------------------------------
Close Status and Tomorrow's Orders
--------------------------------------
Current Positions : SHORT  1 at     382.62 on 06/12/91   (O# 2)

Close Status :  1 SHORT position            Open Equity :    1015.00

Before the open, place the following orders :
  O# 1              : BUY   2  at     382.85  STOP
=================================================================================
S&P 500 Composite      D 03/92                          Fri.   07/05/91
---------------------------------------------------------------------------------
Open :     378.60  High :     383.10  Low :     378.60  Close :     380.80
---------------------------------------------------------------------------------
Trade Summary
-------------------

Trade Order !  Type  ! Entry  !  Price  !! Trade Order ! Type !  Exit   !  Price  !  Net P&L

  O# 2   ! 1 Sell ! 06/12/91 !  382.62 !! O# 1  ! Buy  ! 07/05/91 !  382.85 ! [$  265.00]
                                                      Net Profit/Loss ! [$  265.00]
---------------------------------------------------------------------------------------
```

Figure 10-4   Daily Reports

• 159 •

```
Close Status and Tomorrow's Orders
-------------------------------------
Current Positions : LONG   1 at     382.85 on 07/05/91   (O# 1)

Close Status :  1 LONG position            Open Equity :    -1025.00

Before the open, place the following orders :
  O# 2             : SELL  2   at     374.05  STOP
=================================================================
S&P 500 Composite      D 03/92                    Mon.  07/08/91
-----------------------------------------------------------------
  Open :    378.90  High :      385.10  Low :     377.00  Close :     384.85
-----------------------------------------------------------------
Close Status and Tomorrow's Orders
-------------------------------------
Current Positions : LONG   1 at     382.85 on 07/05/91   (O# 1)

Close Status :  1 LONG position            Open Equity :     1000.00

Before the open, place the following orders :
  O# 2             : SELL  2   at     376.55  STOP
=================================================================
S&P 500 Composite      D 03/92                    Tues.  07/09/91
-----------------------------------------------------------------
  Open :    384.80  High :      385.75  Low :     381.60  Close :     383.20
-----------------------------------------------------------------
Close Status and Tomorrow's Orders
-------------------------------------
Current Positions : LONG   1 at     382.85 on 07/05/91   (O# 1)

Close Status :  1 LONG position            Open Equity :      175.00

Before the open, place the following orders :
  O# 2             : SELL  2   at     375.73  STOP
=================================================================
S&P 500 Composite      D 03/92                    Wed.  07/10/91
-----------------------------------------------------------------
  Open :    384.10  High :      387.80  Low :     381.10  Close :     383.15
-----------------------------------------------------------------
Close Status and Tomorrow's Orders
-------------------------------------
Current Positions : LONG   1 at     382.85 on 07/05/91   (O# 1)

Close Status :  1 LONG position            Open Equity :      150.00

Before the open, place the following orders :
  O# 2             : SELL  2   at     375.33  STOP
=================================================================
S&P 500 Composite      D 03/92                    Thurs.  07/11/91
-----------------------------------------------------------------
  Open :    384.80  High :      385.10  Low :     381.65  Close :     384.90
-----------------------------------------------------------------
Close Status and Tomorrow's Orders
-------------------------------------
Current Positions : LONG   1 at     382.85 on 07/05/91   (O# 1)

Close Status :  1 LONG position            Open Equity :     1025.00

Before the open, place the following orders :
  O# 2             : SELL  2   at     378.95  STOP
=================================================================
S&P 500 Composite      D 03/92                    Fri.  07/12/91
-----------------------------------------------------------------
  Open :    386.10  High :      388.80  Low :     381.75  Close :     387.20
-----------------------------------------------------------------
Close Status and Tomorrow's Orders
-------------------------------------
Current Positions : LONG   1 at     382.85 on 07/05/91   (O# 1)

Close Status :  1 LONG position            Open Equity :     2175.00

Before the open, place the following orders :
  O# 2             : SELL  2   at     379.00  STOP
```

Figure 10-4 *(Continued)*

INDEX